George F Fitzgerald

Lord Kelvin, Professor of natural Philosophy in the University of Glasgow, 1846-1899

With an Essay on his scientific Work

George F Fitzgerald

Lord Kelvin, Professor of natural Philosophy in the University of Glasgow, 1846-1899

With an Essay on his scientific Work

ISBN/EAN: 9783743337596

Manufactured in Europe, USA, Canada, Australia, Japa

Cover: Foto ©Thomas Meinert / pixelio.de

Manufactured and distributed by brebook publishing software (www.brebook.com)

George F Fitzgerald

Lord Kelvin, Professor of natural Philosophy in the University of Glasgow, 1846-1899

This Special Edition was printed at the University Press, Glasgow, November, 1899. Only two hundred copies of it were for sale, and these were all subscribed for before publication.

LORD KELVIN

Professor of Natural Philosophy in the University of Glasgow

1846-1899

With an Essay on his Scientific Work by George F. Fitzgerald Trinity College, Dublin

And an account of the Celebrations on the occasion of Lord Kelvin's Jubilee as a Professor

Glasgow
James MacLehose and Sons
Publishers to the University
1899

List of Illustrations

List of Illustrations

Biographical Sketch of Lord Kelvin

By Professor Fitzgerald

Biographical Sketch

William Thomson, now Lord Kelvin, was born on 26th June, 1824, in Belfast. His father, Professor James Thomson, was a man of great energy and determination, and was distinguished for his abilities as a mathematician and teacher. While a teacher at Ballinahinch, Co. Down, he had attended the University of Glasgow. About 1812 he was appointed a teacher in the Royal Academic Institute in Belfast, and it was during his tenure of this office that his two illustrious sons James and William were born.

By 1832 Professor James Thomson had attained such a wide and established reputation that the University of Glasgow appointed him to the Chair of Mathematics, which he held till his death in 1849.

In 1834 his two sons, James and William, the latter being only a little over ten years of age, matriculated in the University of Glasgow. They had both been educated by their father at home, and some of the originality and power of both these distinguished men is almost certainly due to the individual attention given them by one who was himself in great measure a self-trained teacher, to the enthusiasm for knowledge he imparted, and which was not damped by the sneers of fellow-schoolboys, and to the absence of that bedmoulding that forces the members of a community in a large school into similarity with its prevailing ideas. Variety is as essential for advance as is inheritance. Mankind have the inestimable advantage over other forms of life, that, by the enormous development of tradition, by words and books, and by carefully conducted education, they can largely transmit useful acquired characteristics. The influence of the past being so powerful, it is the more important to cultivate originality, or modern civilisation may degenerate into a Chinese conservativism.

William Thomson studied for six years in classes in the University of Glasgow, but did not take any degree there until 1896, when the University conferred upon him the honorary degree of LL.D., on the occasion of his Jubilee.

In 1841 he proceeded to Cambridge, where he entered St. Peter's College. During his four years' residence at Cambridge he was universally looked upon as one of the coming lights of science. With that unbending regard for the sacredness of "marks" at an examination which characterises that great University, he was awarded second Wranglership in 1845, although it was said of him by a University examiner that the Senior Wrangler "was not fit to cut pencils for Thomson." However, at the subsequent Smith's Prize examination he obtained first place. He was the same year elected fellow of his College. During these years of growth of his physical constitution he took good heed that this important agent of the soul should develop healthily. He rowed so effectively that he won the Colquhoun sculls. Nor did he neglect Art. Music claimed his attention, and he became President of the Musical Society.

During the first half of the present century physical science was largely indebted to French science for its advances. A devotion to Newton that almost amounted to a worship had largely paralysed advance in English Universities. Germany had not effectively developed the methods by which it now floods the world with new knowledge. It was from French inspiration that Thomson drew the food for his thoughts. To Paris he looked for the means of further advance. Although he had been four years at Cambridge, he was not so blinded by his surroundings as not to appreciate the enormous importance of experimental investigation, and to Paris he went for instruction. Here Fourier, Fresnel, Ampère, Arago, Biot, and Regnault showed how to combine experimental induction with mathematical deduction. They were the true disciples of Newton; not those who, like the professed followers of Aristotle, followed tradition rather than the example of their master, and trusted to pen and paper rather than to nature for their inspiration. In Paris he worked in Regnault's laboratory, where classical determinations of physical constants were being made. At this time there were no English laboratories available for students, and it is to Lord Kelvin that we owe the introduction of laboratory work for students into the curricula of our Universities; the greatest advance that has been made in the methods of education for centuries. His year's work in Paris concluded the educational period of his life. He had had experience of three Universities of very distinct types—Glasgow, Cambridge, and Paris—so that his training combined that of a German student, who seeks great teachers wherever they are to be found, with that of an English student, who is more dominated by the spirit of a community than inspired by a prophet.

During the next year, 1846, the Professorship of Natural Philosophy at Glasgow fell vacant, and the University authorities showed their wisdom and their appreciation of true genius by appointing William Thomson, at the age of 22, to this important Professorship. Other Universities have envied Glasgow the possession of such a Professor, but they have never succeeded in tempting him from his allegiance to Glasgow. For fifty-three years then, from 1846 till 1899, he has held this Professorship, and has shed on Glasgow and on all Britain great light, and now retires with the respectful goodwill and admiration of the nation.

His subsequent public career can be most easily traced in the work he has done. For it he was knighted in 1866, and created a peer in 1892. For it foreign governments, universities, and learned societies have honoured themselves and him by conferring on him titles, degrees, medals, honorary memberships, too numerous to mention here. The fount of honour in Britain has not yet taken Faraday's advice of creating an order confined to the leaders of science, whose members should have the same precedence as the aristocracy of other orders. If such an order had been created, William Thomson would have received the precedence of a duke, and Britain is the loser by his not having it.

He has been twice married. First, in 1852, to Miss Margaret Crum, daughter of Walter Crum, Esq., of Thornliebank. She died in 1870. Secondly, in 1874, to Miss Frances Anna Blandy, daughter of Charles R. Blandy, Esq., of Madeira, who, as Lady Kelvin, is honoured and beloved by all who know her.

On reading over the articles published in various journals, at the time of Lord Kelvin's Jubilee, the characteristic of his genius

that is most frequently, indeed universally, noticed is his ability to combine science with practice. These two sides of his activity for mankind may be made the basis of a division of his work. He has published most important papers on a great variety of branches of mathematical physics, and he has made a large number of practical inventions, by which the work of the world is lightened and mankind thereby benefited. It is by no means to be imagined that these two directions of his activity are independent of one another. His inventions are the direct outcome of the most advanced theory. He is a living example of the necessity for theory, in order to advance practice as much as is possible. If we trust to advance by the Laputan method of trying a variety of chance combinations and letting the fittest survive, we shall no doubt advance slowly; but we shall certainly be beaten in the race by those who act on the belief that the highest scientific training will lead to much more rapid advance by utilising the intellectual powers of men in choosing what combinations to try. Without Lord Kelvin's theory as to how signals were transmitted in telegraph cables, it would have taken many years of chance experimenting to evolve the mirror galvanometer.

Lord Kelvin's most important contribution to Mathematical Physics may be classed under the heads of

General Dynamics. Hydrodynamics.
Elasticity. Thermodynamics.
Electromagnetism.

In each of these departments he has left his mark on the science of the nineteenth century. The characteristics of his work have been admirably described by the most competent critic,

Helmholtz, as follows: "His peculiar merit consists in his method of treating problems of mathematical physics. He has striven with great consistency to purify the mathematical theory from hypothetical assumptions which were not a pure expression of the facts. In this way he has done very much to destroy the old unnatural separation between experimental and mathematical physics, and to reduce the latter to a precise and pure expression of the laws of the phenomena. He is an eminent mathematician, but the gift to translate real facts into mathematical equations, and *vice versa*, is by far more rare than that to find a solution of a given mathematical problem, and in this direction Sir William Thomson is most eminent and original."

Lord Kelvin's mathematics is of that specially powerful type that distinguishes giants like Laplace and Green. He is determined, at all costs, to solve the problem, and does not give up because it leads to laborious approximations and complicated series. He rejoices no doubt in elegant methods as, for example, in his theory of electrical images; but sledge-hammer methods are at hand if required to obtain the result. His mathematics is for the sake of the result and not the result for the sake of the mathematics. He has especially developed the methods of physical investigation depending on applications of the principle of the conservation of energy, and the popularity of this method owes a great deal to his powerful example. A generation that has been reared on the ideas involved in the conservation of energy can hardly understand the position of science when Lord Kelvin began his professoriate. Before the equivalence of heat and energy was recognised, when forces were distinguished into conservative and unconservative, when the world was filled with subtile fluids, effluvia, and other hyper-dynamical entities, it must have seemed almost hopeless to look for any general explanation of material phenomena.

The most advancing minds of the times were strongly impressed with the importance of correlating the "forces of nature," as they were called. Light and heat, electricity, magnetism, and chemical activity were all distinct "forces," each a cause of change, but very little had been done in the direction of any explanation of these actions, on what would be now recognised as a dynamical basis. How could a dynamical basis be recognised when the nature of heat even was unknown? Of all these "forces," no doubt, we have still very much to learn, and of chemical activity we know very little indeed, but that a dynamical explanation of them all is possible, and that we are on the proper track for attaining to this result very few indeed now doubt. That we have attained so far is largely due to Lord Kelvin and his work. When he began, mathematical physics in Britain was largely in the hands of those whose tastes and training were purely mathematical. The physical basis of the equations they used was not of much importance to them. They were quite content to take positive and negative electric fluids and magnetic fluids for granted. There was no difficulty in deducing equations from their assumed properties and hence little interest was taken in the question of their real existence. That, in such a fundamental subject as elementary dynamics, it was not generally considered necessary to distinguish between a purely kinematic quantity, such as acceleration, and the force of gravity, shows how careless mathematical physicists then were as to the basis upon which their analysis was raised. Thomson and Tait, by their

"Natural Philosophy," and by the influence of their other teaching, have roused British science from this disastrous position. They emphasised the necessity for an experimental basis of natural philosophy, and for a clear and distinct nomenclature. They took as their text the following quotation from Fourier:

"Les causes primordiales ne nous sont pas connues; mais elles sont assujetties à des lois simples et constantes, que l'on peut découvrer par l'observation, et dont l'étude est l'object de la philosophie naturelle."

They, as far as possible, treated the subject in non-mathematical language, for, as they state in the Preface, "Nothing can be more fatal to progress than a too confident reliance on mathematical symbols; for the student is only too apt to take the easier course, and consider the *formula* not the *fact* as the physical reality."

By referring back to nature for verification and enlightenment, they laid the foundation for a sure advance, and, by clearing away as much as possible all hypothetical assumptions, they went a long way towards breaking down the wall of separation between experimental and mathematical physics. In a work by two authors it is not possible to clearly apportion the credit between them. Certain parts of the "Treatise on Natural Philosophy" are so intimately bound up with Lord Kelvin's other work that it is desirable to specially refer to them. The problem of gyrostatic domination and kinetic stability is one that has throughout his life attracted his attention. It is intimately connected with questions of kinetic elasticity, and any student of Lord Kelvin's work must be impressed with the way in which this idea is continually

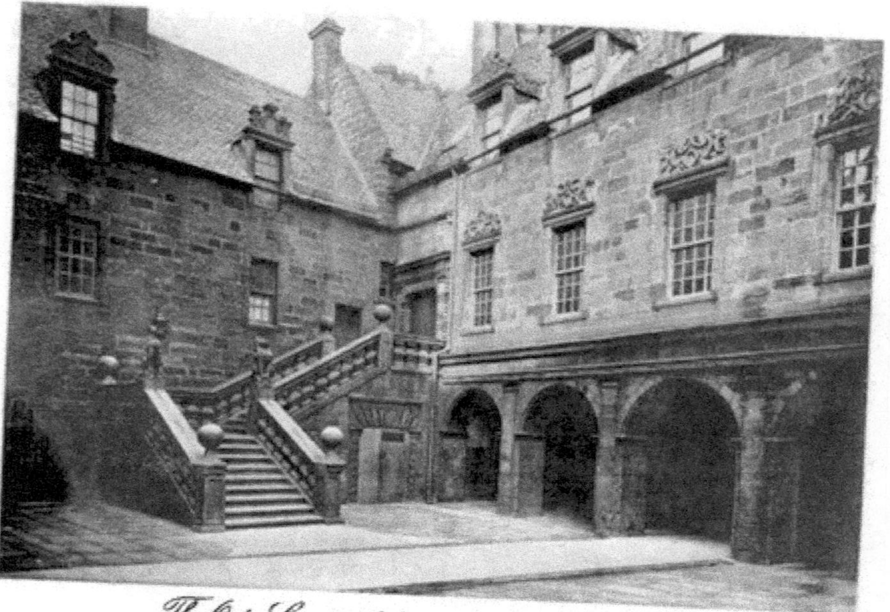

The Outer Court, with the great stair leading to the Fore Hall.

recurring in his papers. Gyroscopes and their vibrations and motions, vortex rings, with their kinetic elasticity, media constructed with gyrostatic elasticity,—these are the subjects of continually recurring thought. It is in this direction that he has made the most strenuous efforts to discover the explanation of electric and magnetic force, the relation between ether, electricity, and ponderable matter, and the nature of chemical affinity. Though he himself has described these efforts as resulting in failure, his contemporaries and disciples see a succession of brilliant successes, which have not, indeed, fully conquered the citadel of ignorance against which they were directed, but have, nevertheless, conquered many and fair districts, and advanced the armies of knowledge in their reconnaissance of this citadel to an extent that was only possible for a great general, an indefatigable and enthusiastic genius.

Directly connected with these gyrostatic problems in Thomson and Tait's "Natural Philosophy" is the general problem of stability of equilibrium. The attack on this problem is directed along the line pointed out by Maupertius, Lagrange, and Hamilton, one of the most important general theorems of abstract dynamics. They demonstrated that what is known as the Principle of Least-Action is true of the whole material world. It is a sufficient foundation for the theory of the planets and satellites of the solar system, of spinning wheels, lathes, machines of all kinds, of every material system in which we can define with accuracy the motions of its parts and the forces acting on them. The problem involved in determining the motions of a system in accordance with this principle is essentially that of determining a minimum. Lord Kelvin, in one of his popular lectures and addresses, delivered as a Friday evening discourse, at the Royal Institution in 1893 brought under the notice of a semi-popular audience the nature and importance of this great dynamical generalisation. This discourse is on Isoperimetrical Problems, and, by a series of interesting concrete cases of the problem of discovering a minimum, including Dido's problem of drawing the shortest line round the most valuable piece of country, of designing a railway line to join two towns through undulating country at the least cost, and other such problems, he brought before his audience the general idea of determining a minimum subject to complex limitations. The nature of the problem will be clear to anybody who follows out the advice given in this memorable discourse, which lays down so clearly the heuristic method of teaching, and, beginning with simple concrete cases, which the learner is exhorted to work out experimentally and synthetically for himself, gradually leads him to generalisations of the widest scope. This is the history of the problem, and it should be the method of learning. It is no easy matter to extend generalisations that have been elaborated by such geniuses as Lagrange and Hamilton, but in his investigation of kinetic foci Lord Kelvin has done this. This is essentially a generalisation of the problem of conjugate foci in optics, and is a remarkable example of Lord Kelvin's splendid gift of discovering the essential similarity between problems apparently the most diverse. Very few would see any connection between Dido's problem of surrounding the most valuable land with a cowhide and the stability of water rotating in an ellipsoidal vessel, yet these are the first and last subjects touched on in this discourse on Isoperimetrical Problems. Similarly, there does not seem much connection between conjugate foci in optics and the motion of a particle inside an anchor ring, and yet these are two of the simplest examples of Lord Kelvin's general theory of kinetic foci.

Elasticity.—The theory of elasticity owes a great deal to Lord Kelvin. In Karl Pearson's great "History of Elasticity" more than a hundred pages are devoted to his contributions to this subject. It is there stated of his work on elasticity, "There is that fertility of idea and that mark of genius which has made Sir William Thomson the leader and characteristic representative of physical science in our own country to-day." One of the most remarkable peculiarities of these contributions is the way in which they bristle with suggestions as to all sorts and kinds of elastic media. To him is due the rejection of a simple elastic solid theory of the ether and the suggestion of a quasi elasticity produced by gyrostatic domination, the elaboration of the whole theory of thermoelasticity, the development of Boscovich's hypothesis into a molecular theory of matter, and, above all, the application of elastic theory to calculate the deformations of the earth by solar and lunar gravitation, and the effect that its elasticity must have upon the tides and on precession and nutation. His treatment of the elasticity of solids has largely influenced the whole British school of elasticians, and his fecundity in devising elastic mechanisms has emphasised his fight against the supposed necessity that, in a simple solid, the rigidity is three-fifths of the compressibility. This may no doubt be used as a definition of a simple solid, but, in that case, hardly any real solids are simple solids, and little or no value can be attached to a relation that is hardly ever of any service. Our knowledge of the structure of matter is far too meagre for us to deduce, *a priori*, such a result, and Lord Kelvin has always advocated the scientific method of proving by induction that, in a large number of cases, we can reduce the elastic properties of a solid to its rigidity and compressibility, and deduce its behaviour under stress from a knowledge of these two qualities.

The application of the theory of an elastic solid to the case of the earth is characteristic of Lord Kelvin. He has no hesitation in applying results deduced from experiments on a small scale to cases where the scale is immensely greater: he seizes at once the conditions of the problem, and applies the overwhelmingly powerful mathematical analysis at his command to its solution. He has specially considered the two questions as to how the elasticity of the materials of which the earth is composed must influence the tides and as to how it must influence precession and nutation. The general result of these cosmic investigations is that the earth is probably about as rigid as steel, but that more careful determinations of long period tides and short period nutations would enable us to decide more accurately than we can at present as to its actual rigidity.

Hydrodynamics.—Hydrodynamics has been a subject of interest to naturalists ever since the times of Hero and Archimedes. Nearly every great worker on mathematical physics has devoted attention to it. Yet it was reserved for comparatively recent times to study one whole and important branch of the subject. The study of vortex motion begins with Helmholtz, and is under the very greatest obligations to Lord Kelvin. He has developed some of the most important general theories in reference to it, and has founded upon it the suggestive hypothesis of the vortex atom. Having

The Inner Court, showing Tower

shown that vortex rings are stable, he has suggested that the atoms of matter may consist of some of the various species of vortex ring in a perfect liquid. They would certainly possess a large number of the essential characteristics of matter, permanence, elasticity, and the ability to act upon one another at a distance; and, though the medium in which all matter is immersed, the ether, is certainly more complex than a merely perfect liquid, and though the atoms of matter are certainly more complex than simple thin vortex rings, yet this hypothesis is the most far-reaching of any that have been proposed as a solution of the problem of the ultimate structure of matter. The origination of this hypothesis and the development of the theory of vortex motions would have alone sufficed to establish a great scientific reputation; but, in addition to his work on vortex motion, Lord Kelvin has worked most fruitfully at other problems in hydrodynamics, such as waves produced by obstacles on a moving liquid, and has, as is being explained in this introduction, made a great scientific reputation in many other branches of physical science. His discussion of the problem of the stability or instability of fluid motion in several important cases, of the way in which fluids become filled with turbulent motion, and of the propagation of waves in vortices and turbulent liquids have opened up immense tracts of territory for exploration. In connection with navigation and with the question as to the rigidity of the earth he has devoted a good deal (for others it would have been a great deal) of his attention to the study of the tides, and has very much facilitated the calculation of tide tables for any given port by his tide calculating machine. This is essentially a machine by which the sum of a Fourier series is obtained by mechanical means. The tides for a whole year can be wound out of it in the space of four hours, thus facilitating the prediction of tides to an extraordinary degree. The form in which it gives the prediction being a continuous curve on paper, it enables the height of the water at any moment to be ascertained by inspection, while any arithmetical result that could possibly be worth the trouble of calculating would only give the times of high and low water. Following up this subject, Lord Kelvin, utilising a mechanical invention of his distinguished brother Professor James Thomson, invented a series of machines for performing mechanically the operation of calculating the solution of a great variety of differential equations, and finally showed how this mechanism might be used to solve any differential equation of any order. It is in the highest degree interesting to see how a machine can be constructed to perform these elaborate mathematical calculations; and they exhibit, in no ordinary way, the genius of their inventor. To the careless observer it might appear as if no intellect were required to perform what a machine can do, but this is to overlook the still higher intellectual ability required to invent the machine.

Thermodynamics.—One of the most remarkable things in scientific history is the extraordinary variety in the rate at which provisional hypotheses disappear after they have been shown to be untenable. It took many years of hard hammering to beat away the "emission hypothesis" scaffolding that had been erected in order to build up our knowledge of light. It hardly took five years to beat away the "caloric hypothesis" when once the axe was wielded by Lord Kelvin. In the beginning of the century the caloric hypothesis had been really disproved by the experiments of Rumford and Davy, but the hypothesis lasted many years after their time. Yet, within a few years after Joule's determination of the mechanical equivalent of heat, the caloric hypothesis was completely given up and the dynamical theory of heat and the conservation of energy were universally accepted. Joule's measurements were at the time almost ridiculed and had few hearty supporters; but, fortunately for science, one of them was Professor Thomson. He seized the great idea, worked out its ramifications into all the corners of the domain of physics, and forced it on British science.

The great stumbling-block in the way of accepting the dynamical theory of heat was the difficulty of accurately defining temperature. Founding on Carnot's work, Lord Kelvin put this matter upon a perfectly satisfactory scientific basis. Before he propounded his absolute scale, purely empirical scales, founded on the behaviour of various gases, liquids and solids, had each its advocate, and there seemed to be no satisfactory reason for preferring one to another. Once he propounded the absolute scale, no question has ever since been raised but that it is the only rational scale to adopt as an absolute one. No matter how much more convenient empirical scales may be, it is recognised that they are only provisional and adapted to supply a temporary need for want of the data required in order to reduce them to the absolute scale. And yet at the time this scale was originally propounded great difficulties surrounded the whole subject. The doctrine of the identity of heat and energy was in direct contradiction to the principles upon which Carnot's work, which Lord Kelvin used, was based. Carnot himself had, as his posthumously published papers prove, seen clearly that his original assumption of the inconvertibility of heat was untenable, and had indicated the direction in which to look for a reconcilement between the new doctrine and his own former work. These papers were not, however, published till years after the whole matter had been cleared up. Professor James Thomson had implicitly used a principle in his deduction of the change of freezing-point of water with pressure, which solved the whole difficulty, and, a little later, Clausius and Lord Kelvin explicitly propounded essentially the same principle in general terms. This discovery of what is known as the Second Law of Thermodynamics is one of the great discoveries of the century, and with his wonted energy and brilliant rapidity of development and generalisation Lord Kelvin worked out the consequences of the discovery into almost every department of the domain of heat. Not content with its application to physical investigations of the laboratory class and of human application, he further developed the consequences of this great generalisation as it affected the life of the solar system, and propounded the general doctrine of the Dissipation of Energy. From this it appears that, so far as we have any knowledge at present, the whole solar system must ultimately die of cold and become as lifeless as the moon is now.

This startling and far-reaching result naturally led to a consideration of a beginning to our present system. The reaction against the believers that geological history had been a series of catastrophies had led to an unreasonable belief in the uniformity of the past history of the earth. The uniformitarians went so far as to hold that it was practically impossible to set any bounds to

Professors Court, looking West

the past history of the earth under conditions which were virtually the same as at present exist. The authority of Laplace and other astronomers was appealed to, to show that there was no known cause why, so far as astronomical calculations could prove, the solar system might not have existed as it is for an indefinite time. Against all this weight of geological authority Lord Kelvin hurled the thunderbolt of his calculations as to the possible age of the earth and sun, as deduced from considerations of their rate of cooling and from the doctrine of the dissipation of energy. Of course, no very precise calculations were possible, and he gave as limits that the surface of the earth may have been hot enough to be uninhabitable 20,000,000 years ago, but that it cannot have been habitable for more than 400,000,000 years. Geologists and biologists fought hard against any limit being placed to the past history of the earth, and, when they had to give up that position, they fought, and some are still fighting, for more time. Nobody, however, now doubts that there is a limit to the age of the earth. Nobody doubts that, so far as we can see, the sun himself will die. The battle has been won by Lord Kelvin. Uniformitarianism has been completely routed.

Electromagnetism.—In the year 1847 Lord Kelvin started the whole modern method of treating electromagnetism. Founding on the ideas as to action by means of a medium that Faraday had been elaborating, Lord Kelvin showed how to illustrate electromagnetic forces by the distortions of an elastic solid. Thus were set rolling the ideas which have fructified into the modern methods of looking at electromagnetism. Lord Kelvin has himself, no doubt, shown that these distortions of an elastic solid cannot explain the electric and magnetic attractions and repulsions which are the principal evidence we have of electromagnetic actions, and that the medium which does cause these forces cannot be a simple elastic solid such as jelly. Nevertheless, this translating of Faraday's idea into a concrete calculable conception was the clue to the labyrinth into whose innermost recesses Lord Kelvin has ever since been penetrating—it was the clue that Maxwell worked at so successfully and which led him to the electromagnetic theory of light. The analytical methods, founded on Green's, that Lord Kelvin has popularised have permeated all modern investigations. His intense craving for a concrete realisation of whatever he dealt with has driven him to seek a dynamical explanation of electromagnetism, and to reduce all its phenomena to numerical measurement. At the time he began to work, each observer quoted his own galvanometer or his own battery, or his own pet wire. Such and such an action "produced a deflection of 5 divisions of my galvanometer." "My electromagnet was wound with 200 turns of fine wire and excited by 20 cells of Callan's battery." Such are the hints given of what quantities were being dealt with. There was no real attempt to reduce the observations to any common numerical scale. The distinction in many quarters between such essentially different quantities as *current* and *voltage* was very hazy indeed. Authorities spoke of "quantity currents" and "intensity currents," as if they were two distinct kinds of current, one of which produced heat and the other shocks. Accurate ideas as to the connection between energy and electromagnetic quantities were the property of very few indeed. All this muddle and want of definiteness was intolerable to Lord Kelvin. He set himself, in the words of Helmholtz, "to purify the mathematical theory from hypothetical assumptions which were not a pure expression of the facts." In this way he reduced the mathematical theory of electromagnetism to a precise and pure expression of the laws of the phenomena.

Having thus reduced the mathematical expression to its simplest form, and having worked out carefully the connection between energy and electromagnetism, he was in a position to reduce electromagnetic phenomena to numerical calculations and to decide what were the best experiments upon which to found the whole system of electromagnetic measurement. And he set himself to the task of making these measures precise with his wonted energy. Gifted with great constructive ability as well as mathematical genius, he designed the necessary instruments, calculated what their indications meant, and led the way to that wonderful development of accurate electromagnetic measurement which is one of the peculiar characteristics of this branch of science. To his influence is largely due the international system of electromagnetic measures which exists as one system in all civilised nations. It is almost impossible to overestimate the value of such a system, coupled as it is with accurate and easy methods of making the measurements, and to Lord Kelvin, more than to any other man, is due the rapid development and adoption of this rational system, and the accuracy and ease with which the measurements can be made. Some good judges have expressed their opinion that the greatest debt that mankind owes to the labours of Lord Kelvin is on account of his work in connection with the introduction and perfecting of the whole system of electromagnetic measurement.

The mere enumeration of the work on electricity and magnetism that Lord Kelvin has produced would occupy many pages. It may be roughly summarised as dealing with:

(*a*) The mathematical theory of electric and magnetic actions.

(*b*) Experiments and instruments connected with electrostatic measurements, sparks in air, and atmospheric electricity.

(*c*) Questions concerning paramagnetic and diamagnetic induction.

In the papers on the theory of electric and magnetic actions we find developed all those beautiful analogies between electromagnetism and fluid motion which have attracted the attention of every student of this branch of science, and which have popularised the methods of treating the whole subject, which are now almost universally employed. Here also is developed the theory of electric images, which has added a beautiful and powerful method to our means of attacking problems of the distribution of electricity and of fluid motion. Here also we find his classical investigations of the phenomena accompanying the transmission of signals along telegraph wires, upon which are founded both his own inventions, by which submarine telegraphy on long lines was made possible, and also all subsequent telegraph practice. In these papers he proved the oscillatory character of the Leyden jar discharge, which is the basis of all Hertz's work and of wireless telegraphy. He also clearly described all the phenomena of the propagation of electric impulses in cables; and, following Kirchhoff, showed that (in addition to the phenomena of transference of electro-

The Exodus from the Old College

magnetic actions that were observed in cables) there must exist a transmission of electromagnetic actions, with a velocity comparable with that of light and of the nature of a true wave propagation, and not that propagation by diffusion which was used in all cable telegraphy. Thus, he laid the foundation for the electromagnetic theory of light.

One of the characteristics of Lord Kelvin's genius is the combination of theoretical and practical ability. He is probably better known for his inventions than for his discoveries. These inventions have been very various. The principal ones may be divided into those relating to:

(*a*) Telegraphy.
(*b*) Electrical measurements.
(*c*) Navigation.

Between 1840 and 1850 telegraphy advanced very rapidly. One expression of those days shows how entirely electric telegraphy has superseded all other methods of communicating by distant signals. Newspaper paragraphs were then headed "By Electric Telegraph." Nobody nowadays talks of *electric* telegraphs: there are no other telegraphs now. After 1850 submarine telegraphy rose into importance, and was extended from narrow to wider channels, as experience was gained. Attention was early directed to the difficulty of reading signals that succeeded one another with rapidity, when transmitted through long submarine cables. A good deal of confusion existed as to the cause of this slowness in signalling. It was mixed up with the question of how long it would take a signal to reach America. A mere delay in time would not have been of any serious importance. Even though each signal took an hour to reach America, it would be of little importance if it were legible when it reached its destination.

Lord Kelvin, quite early in the discussion, pointed out the conditions that determined the possible rapidity with which signals might follow one another in a cable, and still be legible. He showed that, in all ordinary submarine telegraphy, the speed of signalling depended on the resistance and capacity of the cable and that it varied as the square of its length inversely. This effect of the length of the cable was of vital importance in reference to the then proposed Atlantic cable. In 1855, Lardner writes of this: "The sanguine consider the project practicable and its speedy realisation probable; the phlegmatic notice it only with ridicule; men of science generally admit the possibility of the enterprise; while men of finance more than doubt the possibility of a remunerative result." As these latter in large measure controlled the situation, and as the remunerative result ultimately depended on how many messages could be transmitted by the cable per day, the whole possibility of realising Atlantic telegraphy centred round this question. Mr. Whitehouse, who was an enthusiastic believer in the possibility of success, fought manfully against this "law of squares" as it is called, and published the results of experiments that seemed entirely opposed to the law. He said that, if this law were true, Atlantic telegraphy would be impossible. "I can only regard it as a fiction of the schools, a forced and violent adaptation of a principle in physics, good and true under the circumstances, but misapplied here." To this Lord Kelvin replied by reiterating the applicability of the "law of squares" to submarine telegraphy and by showing that the experiments cited really confirmed the law they were supposed to disprove. He further maintained that, notwithstanding the law of squares, Atlantic telegraphy was possible. His study of the theory of signalling in submarine cables convinced him that most of the proposed developments were going in a wrong direction. Enormous electric pressures had been used and the failure of the insulation in the 1858 cable was, with probability, attributed to this.

Lord Kelvin advocated an entire revolution in all this. Instead of the heavy instruments in use, he substituted his reflecting galvanometer, with its tiny needle, hung by a single silk fibre and its mirror-reflected beam of light to make the movements of the needle visible. He showed that the condition for rapid signalling consisted in being able to observe the first beginnings of the electric current at the far end and to stop the current immediately it had risen to this observable value. To attain these ends he invented the delicate reflecting galvanometer, and subsequently the syphon recorder, and suggested what is known as "curb sending," the effect of which is to stop the current from continuing to increase after it has attained an observable value, thus enabling a second signal to be transmitted shortly after the first. It has been stated by a recognised authority on telegraphy, "the siphon recorder, with its shifting zero, was supremely indifferent to the vagaries of the current which were so destructive of intelligible marks in a dot and dash instrument." These inventions, which rapidly revolutionised submarine telegraph practice and indeed made long distance submarine telegraphs financially successful and consequently possible, were the result of Lord Kelvin's study of the theory of signalling in cables and are a notable example of an invention founded on abstruse mathematical investigation.

In connection with the development of the system of electromagnetic measures, Lord Kelvin has invented a large number of instruments which enable these measurements to be made with facility and accuracy. In order to be able to measure electrostatic forces, he produced the quadrant electrometer and the guardring electrometer: the first enabling observers to measure with accuracy the electrostatic forces due to such small electric pressures as fractions of a volt, and the second enabling them to determine the numerical value, in accordance with a scientific system, of an electric pressure and of a quantity of electricity. Before the invention of these instruments, the measurement of electrostatic quantities was quite arbitrary. Gold leaf electroscopes and other such arbitrary and uncertain instruments were the ones almost universally employed. Coulomb, no doubt, had used his torsion electrometer to good purpose and it could be used to make electric measurements in accordance with a definite system, but the instrument was a most unsatisfactory one to work with and the calculations involved, in comparing its indications with theory, were most difficult and intricate. In electrostatic work, Lord Kelvin's inventions are the basis upon which all subsequent measuring instruments have been designed and to him is due the credit of rescuing this department of electrical measurement from the chaos of arbitrary units. A great development of our knowledge of electrochemical pressures, of the pressure in the neighbourhood of different materials in contact with one another, and of atmospheric electricity has resulted from his and other

West Quadrangle, looking South East

persons' investigations which depended upon the use of these instruments.

Another direction in which his inventive genius has improved the resources of mankind is in producing instruments by which conveniently and accurately the electric currents and pressures that are used in engineering work on a large scale can be measured. He has designed apparatus of all sorts and kinds for measuring, recording, and integrating electric currents; electro-magnetic and electrostatic instruments for measuring and recording electric pressures, and others for measuring electric power. A great many of these instruments are in practical use, and no laboratory or electric-power station would be complete without some of his very beautiful and accurate instruments for measuring electric currents and pressures, in which the forces produced by electric currents are weighed. Lord Kelvin has introduced into instrument-making the use of rational constraints instead of the forced fitting that most designers of accurate adjustments employ, thus increasing the real accuracy of the instrument and, in many cases, increasing, at the same time, its facility of adjustment and use.

The Atlantic Telegraph was rendered possible by Lord Kelvin's inventions, and by his assistance and advice in the innumerable difficulties that were continually arising during the manufacture and laying of the cables. The necessity for his presence on board ships attracted his attention to navigation, to which he has contributed a great deal in addition to his work on the Tides already referred to. In two directions especially has he made important inventions in aid of navigation: he improved the mariner's compass and the navigational sounding apparatus. The introduction of iron as the material of which ships were constructed interfered in a very serious way with the compass by which the ship had to be steered. Some ships are so strongly magnetic that a compass on board would point more nearly to a fixed point on the ship than to a fixed point on the globe. Before Lord Kelvin attacked the problem of designing a good form of compass, innumerable patents had been taken out for all sorts and kinds of compasses, but in practically all of them it was attempted to produce steadiness and certainty of pointing by the employment of large and powerful magnet needles. There is great difficulty in correcting the effect of the iron in the ships on a large magnet: the correcting apparatus would have to be large and placed at a considerable distance from the compass. Lord Kelvin solved the double difficulty of attaining steadiness and ease of correction by making the whole compass card extremely light, with the least material that would secure rigidity, concentrated as far as possible at the circumference of the card, and with small light needles placed near the centre of suspension. By this distribution of the material he ensured a very slow period of vibration for the needle, which produced steadiness; by the very small amount of the material he secured great lightness and consequently very small friction on its pivot, and thus certainty of pointing; while, by the small magnetic needle system, he secured the possibility of correcting for the ship's disturbing influence, by means of a small and easily adjusted system of correctors. The almost universal adoption of these compasses has proved the genius of their inventor.

By his method of sounding from a ship running at full speed by a sinker of from 20 to 30 lbs. weight, carried by strong steel wire (pianoforte wire originally). Lord Kelvin has notably aided navigators in determining their position while still in deep water and at safe distance from rocks or shore. In this method, the greatest vertical depth of the sinker beneath the surface is recorded by an instrument measuring the water-pressure, and is read after it has been brought back on board ship. In the old method of casting the lead the depth is determined from the length of rope run out. With the old method a ship has to be brought to a standstill if any trustworthy measure is to be obtained in deep water: with Lord Kelvin's apparatus, the ship may be running at 20 knots or faster. The value of being able to sound without stopping the ship, or without even reducing its speed, is very important for all ocean-going steamers; and safety at sea in thick weather has been greatly increased by this invention.

The power of intellect is small compared with that of character. Knowledge is power, but Love is omnipotent. Few men's influence is confined to that exerted by their intellect, and, in the case of Lord Kelvin, the influence of his character has been very great indeed, both in his capacity as a teacher and as a leader in the scientific world. His single-minded and enthusiastic devotion to truth has fired the enthusiasm and directed the energies of many disciples. His high ideals of life have raised those of the whole scientific world who look to him as their leader. It is a greater blessing for mankind than any mere intellectual triumph can confer when its intellectual leaders, who command followers by their intellectual pre-eminence, are leaders whose moral ideas are high, and Lord Kelvin is eminently such a one. Enthusiastic for truth, sincere in all his dealings, sympathetic and helpful to all who are thrown in his way, fair and unprejudiced in his judgments of others, thoughtful and loving, his character is such that his disciples venerate and love as well as admire him, and the whole of science is the better for such a leader.

Lord Kelvin's ideals are best gathered from his acts, but may also be gathered from his speeches. What is his idea of "a treasure of which no words can adequately describe the value"? It is "goodwill, kindness, friendship, sympathy, encouragement for more work." What is his ideal condition for happiness? "To live among friends." Whom does he describe as deserving of honour? Those who spend their lives in hardships and dangers fighting for their country, or struggling to do good among the masses of our population, or working for the benefit of the people, in public duty, voluntarily accepted. We rightly feel gratitude to those who, by the conditions of their work, prove their disinterested devotion to duty. But surely all those are equally deserving of our gratitude who work enthusiastically and successfully for the benefit of mankind, even though, in working out their ideals and in benefitting others, they are so admirably constituted as to take a keen delight in their work, which is twice blessed, blessing him that gives and him that takes.

Rightly, the scientific world loves and admires such a leader. He has provided us with magnificent and helpful ideas as to the past and as to the future, as to the immeasurably great and the immeasurably small. He has advanced civilisation by making the all-pervading ether available for our use, by enabling us to measure its properties, and by teaching us how to lay the nerves of civilisation

Professors' Houses, looking South West.

in the depths of the ocean. Above all, he has held up before us a noble ideal of life, he has helped to unify humanity, to modify competition by co-operation, to push forward the federation of the world.

GEORGE F. FITZGERALD.

Trinity College, Dublin.

Celebration of Jubilee of Lord Kelvin

15th, 16th, and 17th June, 1896

The New College, Glasgow

Celebration of Jubilee of Lord Kelvin

THERE can be few old students of Glasgow University who remember the induction of William Thomson to the professorship of Natural Philosophy in 1846. Among the Professors of to-day there is not one who was then even a student at Glasgow. Since Professor Lushington's retirement in 1874 Lord Kelvin has been the senior among his colleagues, and there is the long gap of sixteen years between his appointment in 1846, and that, in 1862, of Sir William Gairdner, who ranks next in seniority. But it was not because of a long life spent at one post that these celebrations were organised.

It was because of the unique character of the work done and of the personality of the worker that the Jubilee of Lord Kelvin became one of the most strangely impressive functions. It had in it something of the nature of a spontaneous outburst of enthusiasm, as well as of the studied and respectful homage shown by representatives of all the world to a great thinker and actor. At the gatherings held in the University and in the City of Glasgow in 1896 to signalise the fiftieth year of Lord Kelvin's tenure of the chair of Natural Philosophy in the University of Glasgow, no element in our academic or national life was left unrepresented. Delegates from every seat of learning and from nearly every scientific body in Great Britain and Ireland were assembled, and with them were the men who have made or are making their mark in Glasgow and in the West of Scotland. Representatives there were too from the Colonies, and many brilliant and distinguished foreigners came to do honour to their great scientific fellow-worker.

The students at the University had invited delegates from the Universities of Great Britain and Ireland, and from many foreign Universities as well, and throughout the Celebrations it was evident that the undergraduates were as eager to honour their senior professor as were his oldest friends. It was interesting also to notice that among the great number of congratulatory messages received by Lord Kelvin during this week, there were many from men who had formerly been undergraduates in his class, and who now occupy posts in various parts of the world. As an instance of this may be mentioned the addresses sent from former Japanese students in Lord Kelvin's class, now at Tokyo. And this was in part because his students had always felt that Lord Kelvin was as youthful in spirit and as full of energy as any undergraduate. In 1891, at a College meeting, he said, "I have been a student of the University of Glasgow fifty-five years to-day, and I hope to continue a student of the University as long as I live"; and in 1899, when he retired from his Professorship, he applied to the Senatus Academicus to be appointed a Research Student. His name will therefore still appear on the College Roll, and in the list of those who have the right to pursue investigations in the Natural Philosophy Laboratory.

Conversazione at the University

The first gathering, a conversazione in the halls of the University, took place on the evening of Monday, June 15, 1896.

It was a brilliant sight, and very different from the daily routine of Academic life. The sombre halls and cloisters and staircases of the College were lit up by electric light, decorated with flowers, and filled with a moving mass of colour; and the summer evening was so beautiful that in the eastern quadrangle many of the guests strolled up and down listening to the pipes of the Gordon Highlanders. The innumerable differences in the robes worn by the guests represented well the cosmopolitan character of the gathering.

About two thousand five hundred ladies and gentlemen had been invited, embracing the representatives of Universities, Societies, and Institutions, and other distinguished visitors; the members of the University Court and Senate, about four hundred and fifty members of the General Council, and fully two hundred Students; the Lord Provost, Magistrates, and members of the Town Council, and many prominent citizens of Glasgow and residents in the West of Scotland and other parts of the country. The Bute Hall, the Hunterian Museum, and the upper hall of the Library were thrown open, and in the latter there was an exhibition of mechanical, electrical, and scientific apparatus and contrivances designed by Lord Kelvin;

and of the diplomas and certificates of membership, as well as medals, presented to him by Universities, Colleges, and Institutions.

In the upper hall of the Library the Eastern, the Anglo-American, and the Commercial Cable Companies had fitted up syphon-recorders in connection with their cables, and a large number of congratulatory telegrams from all parts of the world were received in the course of the evening, and suitable replies transmitted. But perhaps the most interesting telegram was the one which, sent from the College, reached Lord Kelvin, after seven minutes and a half, by way of Newfoundland, New York, Chicago, San Francisco, Los Angeles, New Orleans, Florida, Washington, New York, and Newfoundland. The distance covered by the message was about twenty thousand miles. Lord Kelvin sent a reply thanking the Jubilee Arrangements Committee for their good wishes, and this message, sent by the same circuitous route, returned to the Library of the University in four minutes.

In addition to this message there were many other telegrams received during the evening from all parts of the world, and among others from the Viceroy of India, the Governor of Hong Kong, the Premier of Natal, and the Postmaster-General of New Zealand.

After the Conversazione the Students held a Gaudeamus and a reception of delegates from other Universities in the large hall of the Union.

Presentation of Addresses

On Tuesday morning, June 16, 1896, an impressive function took place in the Bute Hall of the University, when the many distinguished men assembled in Glasgow presented to Lord Kelvin addresses from the Universities and Societies whom they represented. A letter was first read from the Prince of Wales.

MARLBOROUGH HOUSE,
10th June, 1896.

DEAR LORD KELVIN,

The Prince of Wales desires me to offer you his warmest congratulations upon your having attained the fiftieth year of the tenure of your professorship in the University of Glasgow.

His Royal Highness is in most cordial sympathy with the eminent representatives of universities, learned societies, and other public bodies in different parts of this empire and in foreign states, who, to do you honour, have assembled in the University which has for a long series of years—eventful through the rapid advance of science and its applications—enjoyed the high prestige derived from your close association with its work, and from the invaluable and brilliant contributions to science resulting from the researches carried on by you during the last half century within its walls.

The Prince of Wales remembers with much satisfaction that he had the gratification, seventeen years ago, to present you with the medal instituted by the Society of Arts as a memorial of the Prince Consort, and awarded to men who have rendered pre-eminent service in promoting arts, manufactures, and science.

The work which you had at that time accomplished was but an earnest of the important researches to which you have since then devoted yourself so indefatigably, and he cherishes the sincere hope that you may long continue to enjoy the happiness derived from the most gratifying evidence that the high value of the service rendered by you through science to mankind is universally recognised and appreciated.

I remain, Dear Lord Kelvin,

Yours truly,

FRANCIS KNOLLYS.

P.S.—His Royal Highness desires me to repeat what he has already stated to the University authorities, how greatly he regrets that long formed engagements in the south prevent him from having the pleasure of being present on the occasion of this interesting celebration.

FRANCIS KNOLLYS.

Thereafter the following Congratulatory Addresses were presented to Lord Kelvin at the public Ceremonial in the Bute Hall on Tuesday, 16th June, 1896:—

I.—FROM UNIVERSITIES.

Aberdeen—University of

Presented by Professor Finlay, M.D., Professor Niven, F.R.S., and Professor Pirie.

Ann Arbor—University of Michigan

Presented by Professor R. M. Wenley, M.A., D.Sc., D.Phil.

Baltimore—Johns Hopkins University

Presented by James C. Thomas, M.D.

Bombay—University of

Presented by Mr. Justice Jardine, Vice-Chancellor, and G. N. Nadkarin, LL.B.

Cambridge—University of

Presented by Professor A. R. Forsyth, Sc.D., F.R.S., Professor Sir George G. Stokes, LL.D., D.C.L., F.R.S., and Professor J. J. Thomson, M.A., F.R.S.

Edinburgh—University of

Presented by Professor Crum Brown, M.D., F.R.S., and Professor Sir William Turner, LL.D., D.C.L., F.R.S.

Glasgow University—Senatus Academicus

Presented by Professor Stewart, D.D.

Glasgow University—General Council

Presented by John G. Kerr, M.A., and Archibald Craig, LL.B.

Heidelberg—University of

Presented by Professor Quincke.

Kasan—Imperial University of

Lille—University of

Presented by Professors Pinloche and Angellier.

London—University of
Presented by Sir Henry E. Roscoe, F.R.S., Vice-Chancellor, and Professor Carey Foster, F.R.S.

Montreal—M'Gill University
Presented by Sir D. A. Smith, G.C.M.G., LL.D., Chancellor, and W. Peterson, LL.D., Principal.

New Haven, Conn.—Yale University

New York—Columbia University
Presented by Professor Van Amringe.

Oxford—University of
Presented by Professor Clifton, F.R.S., D. B. Monro, M.A., Provost of Oriel, and Professor Burdon Sanderson, F.R.S.

Paris—University of

Paris—Theological Faculty of University of
Presented by Professor Bonet-Maury.

Philadelphia—University of Pennsylvania
Presented by Professor G. F. Barker, M.D.

Princeton, New Jersey—University of
Presented by Professor Woodrow Wilson.

Rome—University of
Presented by General Annibale Ferrero.

St. Andrews—University of
Presented by Professor Pettigrew, M.D., LL.D., F.R.S., and Professor Scott Lang.

Sydney—University of
Presented by Professor Liversidge, M.A., F.R.S.

Tokyo—Imperial University of Japan

Upsala—University of
Presented by Professor P. T. Cleve.

Victoria University
Presented by Principal Ward, Vice-Chancellor, and Professors Lodge, Osborne Reynolds, M'Cunn, and Stroud.

Wales—University of
[Signed by Prince of Wales as Chancellor.]
Presented by Principal Viriamu Jones and Professor Andrew Gray, LL.D., F.R.S.

Washington—Columbian University
Presented by Professor Cleveland Abbe.

II.—FROM COLLEGES.

Aberystwith—University College
Presented by R. D. Roberts, M.A., D.Sc.

Bangor—University College of North Wales
Presented by Professor Andrew Gray, LL.D., F.R.S.

Belfast—Queen's College
Presented by Rev. Thomas Hamilton, D.D., LL.D., President, and Professor Purser, LL.D.

Cork—Queen's College
Presented by Professor Bergin, M.A.

Dublin—Royal College of Science for Ireland

Galway—Queen's College
Presented by Sir Thomas Moffett, LL.D.

London—City and Guilds Technical College, Finsbury
Presented by Professor Sylvanus P. Thompson, D.Sc., F.R.S.

London—Royal College of Science
Presented by Professor W. A. Tilden, D.Sc., F.R.S.

London—University College
Presented by Professor Ramsay, F.R.S.

Newcastle-on-Tyne—Durham College of Science
Presented by Professor Philipson, M.D.

Oxford—Balliol College—Master and Scholars

Paris—Ecole Normale Supérieure
Presented by Professor Violle.

III.—FROM SOCIETIES AND INSTITUTIONS

Amsterdam—Royal Academy of Science

Baltimore—Members of Sir William Thomson's (Lord Kelvin's) Class of 1884 at Johns Hopkins University
Presented by Professor Cleveland Abbe.

Berlin—Royal Prussian Academy of Sciences

Cambridge—Bachelors and Undergraduates of University of
Presented by F. W. Lawrence, B.A., and Philip W. Wilson.

Christiania—Students of the University of
Presented by Cato Aall.

Copenhagen—Royal Danish Society of Sciences
Presented by Professor Christiansen.

Cracow—Academy of Letters

Dublin—Science and Art Department

Edinburgh—Educational Institute of Scotland
Presented by John Dunlop, F.E.I.S.

Edinburgh—Scottish Geographical Society
Presented by Sir Renny Watson.

Erlangen—Physikalisch-medicinische Societät zu Erlangen.

Glasgow—Faculty of Physicians and Surgeons
Presented by Bruce Goff, M.D., President.

Glasgow—Geological Society
Presented by Sir Archibald Geikie, F.R.S., and J. Barclay Murdoch, Esq.

Glasgow—School Board of
Presented by Sir John N. Cuthbertson, LL.D., and Rev. William Boyd, LL.D.

Glasgow—Students of University of
Presented by John S. Thomson, President of the Students' Representative Council.

Göttingen—Royal Society of Science
Presented by Professor Woldemar Voigt.

Helsingfors (Finland)—Society of Sciences

Leige—L'Association des Ingénieurs Electriciens Sortis de l'Institut Montefiore

Lille—Students of University of

London—Royal Society
Presented by Sir Joseph Lister, M.B., P.R.S.

London—British Association for Advancement of Science
Presented by Professor A. W. Rücker, F.R.S

London—Royal Institution of Great Britain
Presented by Professor Dewar, F.R.S.

London—Mathematical Society
Presented by Major P. A. MacMahon, R.A., F.R.S.

London—Royal Astronomical Society
Presented by A. Ainslie Common, LL.D., F.R.S.

London—Physical Society
Presented by Captain W. de W. Abney, F.R.S.

London—Chemical Society
Presented by Professor John M. Thomson.

London—Institute of Chemistry of Great Britain and Ireland
Presented by Professor Ramsay, F.R.S.

London—Institution of Electrical Engineers
Presented by John Hopkinson, F.R.S.

London—Institution of Civil Engineers
Presented by Sir Benjamin Baker, K.C.M.G., F.R.S.

London—Society of Engineers
Presented by Henry O'Connor, Esq.

London—Society for Encouragement of Arts, Manufactures, and Commerce

London—Glasgow University Club

Manchester—Literary and Philosophical Society
Presented by Professor Schuster, F.R.S.

Milan—Reale Instituto Lombardo di Scienze e Lettere
Presented by General Annibale Ferrero.

Modena—Royal Academy of Science, Letters, and Arts
Presented by General Annibale Ferrero.

Montreal—Canadian Society of Civil Engineers
Presented by James Ross, Esq.

Moscow—Imperial Society of Naturalists
Presented by Professor Oumov.

Munich—Der Königliche Bayerischen Akademie der Wissenschaften

Newcastle-on-Tyne—Students of Durham College of Science

New-York—National Electric Light Association of America
Presented by Thomas C. Martin, Esq.

Paris—Conservatoire National des Arts et Métiers
Presented by Professor Violle.

Philadelphia—American Philosophical Society
Presented by Dr. J. Cheston Morris.

Rome—Italian Society of Science
Presented by General Annibale Ferrero.

Rome—R. Accademia dei Lincei
Presented by General Annibale Ferrero.

Rotterdam—Batavian Society of Experimental Philosophy
Presented by Dr. Elie van Rijckevorsel.

Scottish Amicable Life Assurance Society.
Signed by Colin Dunlop, Chairman.

Scottish Universities—Students of the four
Presented by J. R. Hunter, Edinburgh University.

Tokyo—Former Students from Japan in Lord Kelvin's Class, now at Tokyo

Vienna—Imperial Academy of Sciences

Washington—National Academy of Sciences
Presented by Professor Simon Newcomb.

Washington—Philosophical Society

It is impossible to give at length the text of all the addresses mentioned in this list, but the following representative ones are of special interest:

From the Royal Society.

Dear Lord Kelvin,—The President, Council and Fellows of the Royal Society desire on the happy occasion of the Jubilee of your Professoriate in the University of Glasgow not only to be represented, as they are, by their highest Officers the President and Treasurer, but also to assure you, by some direct words, of the warm sympathy of the whole Society.

There is no need to dwell on the many ways in which you have contributed to that improvement of natural knowledge to secure which the Society was founded, or on the many valuable communications with which you have enriched the Society's records. Since you first joined the Society, and the Jubilee of that event is not far off, the Society has always known how much your belonging to it has added to its strength; but it has been especially during the recent five years, which went too swiftly by, while you filled in so admirable a manner the chair of President, that the Society has felt how close are the ties which bind it to you and you to it.

We ask you to receive our heartiest congratulations on the present glad event, and our warmest wishes for your welfare in the years yet to come.

JOSEPH LISTER, *President.*

From the Institution of Electrical Engineers.

We, the President, Council, and Members of the Institution of Electrical Engineers, desire hereby to offer to your Lordship our sincere and hearty congratulations on the occasion of the Jubilee of your Professorship of Natural Science in the University of Glasgow. It will ever be a source of pride and satisfaction to this Institution, that one who occupies so pre-eminent a position in the scientific world should have been its First President in 1889, besides having been an original member and President in 1874 of the same Association when it existed under the name of the Society of Telegraph Engineers. Not only have you contributed more than any other living man to our knowledge of the laws of nature, but you have found time to perfect practical applications of Science, wherefrom every branch of the Electrical Engineering Profession has derived special benefit. We desire in conclusion to express our fervent wish that you may continue for many years to enjoy the blessing of good health, and that Science may still further benefit from your labours.

J. HOPKINSON, *President.*
F. H. WEBB, *Secretary.*

From the British Association for the Advancement of Science.

My Lord,—The Council of the British Association for the Advancement of Science desire to offer to you their sincere congratulations on the completion of the fiftieth year of your tenure of the Professorship of Natural Philosophy in the University of Glasgow.

It is unnecessary to recount the triumphs you have won during the last half century in mastering the difficulties which beset the advance of scientific theory and experiment, and in applying scientific principles to the practical service of man. The record of your achievements is fresh in the minds of those who address you, and can never be effaced from the history of the development of mathematical and experimental physics, of engineering, and of navigation. We would rather therefore recall the long and close connection which has existed between the British Association and yourself.

A regular attendant at our meetings, you have not only enriched our reports with many important papers, but have encouraged the efforts of younger men by never-failing sympathy and interest in their work.

You have been President of the Mathematical and Physical Section of the Association no less than five times. You were President of the Association at Edinburgh in 1871, and have since then been a Life Member of our Council.

As colleagues then, we wish to tell you of the pride with which we, in common with all your fellow-countrymen, regard your distinguished career; and of the feelings of personal attachment with which we express the hope that you may long be spared to enjoy in health and strength the honours you have so nobly won.

Signed on behalf of the Council,

DOUGLAS GALTON.

From the University of Edinburgh.

Dear and Honoured Colleague,—It is with feelings of genuine pride and satisfaction, and not as a mere conventional act of courtesy, that we offer you our warmest congratulations on the attainment of your Jubilee as Professor of Natural Philosophy in the University of Glasgow.

We do not attempt to sketch your illustrious career, but we cannot refrain from referring to a few of its grandest features. Second Wrangler, but First Smith's Prizeman, at the age of twenty-one, and appointed to your chair only one year later, you have richly fulfilled the promise of these early successes. During fifty years of zealous and unflagging work your genius has manifested itself at once in theory and in practice. Your contributions to Physics, from the experimental scarcely less than from the theoretical side, have raised you to an all but unique position among men of Science; while your application of scientific principles and (above all) of common sense to the improvement of such indispensable instruments as the Lead-line and the Compass have won for you the applause and the gratitude of the civilised world.

We know not whether most to admire in you the acute Mathematician, the unwearied Investigator of Physical Problems, the skilled Electrician, or the resourceful Engineer; to you in all of these capacities is due the success of Long-line Submarine Telegraphy, with the innumerable benefits resulting from the power of practically instantaneous communication between all parts of the globe.

We are grateful for the lustre which your brilliant discoveries have shed upon our Scottish Universities, and we are proud to number you among our Colleagues.

Abundantly may God bless you and your work: long may He preserve to us your life with its promise of future achievement!

In name and by authority of the Senatus Academics,

For Principal Sir WILLIAM MUIR, K.C.S.I., LL.D., &c.
P. G. TAIT, Senior Professor.
JOHN KIRKPATRICK, Secretary.

From the Master and Scholars of Balliol College, Oxford.

My Lord,—The close connection of Balliol College with the University of Glasgow makes it fitting that we should, on this occasion, give special expression to the deep feelings of respect and admiration which we entertain towards your Lordship.

The long and brilliant career of discovery which has placed you in the front rank of the scientific men of this century it is needless for us to attempt to describe, but we venture to refer to one remarkable and almost unique characteristic of it—namely, that it has been equally distinguished for the profundity and originality of its achievements in the field of abstract mathematical and physical science, and for the ingenuity and inventive power with which the principles of science have been turned to practical uses. This rare combination of gifts constitutes a double claim to the gratitude of all who share in the theoretical and practical benefits of science, and we believe that it will give your name a high and permanent place among those who have contributed to the advances of civilisation and the improvement of the condition of man.

For these reasons we wish to join our voice to the many congratulations which you are now receiving from every part of the civilised world, and to express our hope that you may still have many years to enjoy the regard of your friends and of all who can appreciate your work and to make still further contributions to scientific discovery and invention.

In token whereof we have affixed to this letter our college seal.

Signed in name of the College,

EDWARD CAIRD, *Master.*

From the Master and Fellows of Peterhouse, Cambridge.

To the Right Honourable Lord Kelvin,—We the Master and Fellows of Peterhouse, on the occasion of the Jubilee of your Professorship of Natural Philosophy in the University of Glasgow, desire to express our profound admiration of the splendid discoveries in physical science, and of the valuable scientific inventions, which have characterised the tenure of your professorship and have conferred signal benefits upon the whole civilised world; as well as our gratification and pride that your name, so indissolubly connected with the progress of science in the nineteenth century, should have been for a period of fifty-five years closely connected with this ancient college as Student, Scholar, Fellow, again Fellow *honoris causa* and Benefactor.

We recall with pleasure your noble enthusiasm as an undergraduate in the pursuit of your mathematical studies, and your important contributions to scientific journals, which led our late Master, Dr. Cookson, and your private Tutor, Mr. W. Hopkins, also a distinguished member of the College, at that early period of your career to predict your future eminence in science, and your keen interest in manly sports shown by your success as an oarsman in winning the Colquhoun Sculls, and in rowing in the College boat, which then occupied the second place on the river.

Many of us, students in your Natural Philosophy Class in the University of Glasgow, have enjoyed the privilege of listening to your inspiring lectures; all of us, as your colleagues in the governing body of Peterhouse, have warmly appreciated your unfailing courtesy, wise councils and generous sympathy with all that concerns the welfare of the College. We bear in grateful remembrance your munificence on the occasion of the celebration of the Six Hundredth Anniversary of the foundation of our most ancient House.

We fervently pray that your connection with the College may long continue.

In testimony whereof, we have attached our common seal this thirteenth day of June, in the year of our Lord, One thousand eight hundred and ninety-six.

From the Students of the University of Glasgow.

THE RIGHT HONOURABLE LORD KELVIN,
LL.D. D.C.L. M.D. Ph.D.

PAST PRESIDENT OF THE ROYAL SOCIETY.
PRESIDENT OF THE ROYAL SOCIETY OF EDINBURGH.
PAST PRESIDENT OF THE BRITISH ASSOCIATION.
PAST PRESIDENT OF THE INSTITUTION OF ELECTRICAL ENGINEERS.
GRAND OFFICER OF THE LEGION OF HONOUR OF FRANCE.
KNIGHT OF THE ORDER "POUR LE MERITE" OF GERMANY.
COMMANDER OF THE ORDER OF LEOPOLD OF BELGIUM.
FOREIGN ASSOCIATE OF THE FRENCH ACADEMY.

My Lord,—In the name of the Students of the University of Glasgow we desire to offer you our sincere and hearty congratulations on the occasion of your Jubilee as Professor of Natural Philosophy in our University. While we feel it needless to dwell upon your pre-eminence in the world of science, and would not presume to speak of that genius which has enriched humanity by so many brilliant discoveries, we ask, simply as your students, to be allowed to take our part in the universal congratulation at this time.

We rejoice to have an opportunity of expressing in your presence a feeling of affectionate regard no less strong than the admiration to which others besides ourselves are to-day giving voice.

Above all we desire to refer to your long unbroken connection with our University, a connection which must be endeared to you by many precious memories, and has been to successive generations of students a source of grateful pride. We are proud to think that, year after year, and decade after decade, our University has shared in your ever increasing fame, and that for so long a period it has been her happiness to retain in her midst one whom all nations have delighted to honour.

JOINT COMMITTEE:

From Students' Representative Council.

J. SCOULER THOMSON, *President.*
President Joint Committee.

HYAM GOODMAN, *Hon. Sec.*
Hon. Sec. Joint Committee.

A. J. FLEMING.
JOHN L. TULLOCH.
JOHN MUIR.
DAVID J. YOUNG.

From University Union.

WM. CRAIG HENDERSON, *President*
JOHN C. MONTEITH, *Hon. Sec.*
JOSHUA FERGUSON.
ALEXANDER MACPHAIL.
A. M'CALLUM SCOTT.
W. M. R. PRINGLE.

16th May 1896.

The last address that was presented was

From the Senatus Academicus of the University of Glasgow.

My Lord,—The rejoicings which have been arranged to celebrate the close of your fiftieth session betoken the admiration and affection with which you are regarded by your colleagues in the Senate, but it is none the less fitting that on this auspicious occasion these feelings should find articulate expression in an address of congratulation.

The fifty years during which you have occupied the chair of Natural Philosophy in this University have to an extent unparalleled in the history of the world been marked by brilliant discoveries in every department of Physical Science, and by the prompt adaptation of many of these discoveries to meet the practical needs of mankind. We recognise with admiration that in both these respects you have been a leader of the age in which we live. Your mathematical and experimental genius has unveiled the secrets of nature; your marvellous gift of utilising such discoveries has ministered in many ways to the happiness and dignity of human life. Your name and your work have been an inspiration to the physicists of the world; new departments of technical industry have sprung into existence under your hand; and even the unlettered have learned to value the gifts which Science bestows. The justice of the tributes which have been paid to you by Universities and Scientific Societies at home and abroad, and by the governments of this and other lands, we are proud to acknowledge. But only your colleagues in University work are in a position to appreciate the versatility of faculty, the exhaustless energy, and the tenacity of purpose which have enabled you to grapple successfully with problems the most varied, and to reveal to us on every side the reign of order and law. In the midst of all, you have endeared yourself to us by the graces of your personal character, notably by that simplicity which, unmarred by honours or success, remains the permanent possession of transcendent genius, and by that humility of spirit which, the clearer the vision of truth becomes, bows with the lowlier reverence before the mystery of the universe.

My Lord, the contemplation of a past so rich in achievements and honours encourages your colleagues to look forward to the future in the hope that you may have health and strength to win new triumphs in years to come, and long to remain among us the ornament and the glory of our ancient University.

WILLIAM STEWART,
Clerk of Senate.

Then followed the giving of degrees. In the absence of Principal Caird, through illness, Sir William Gairdner K.C.B., Professor of the Practice of Medicine, occupied the chair in the earlier part of the meeting during the presentation of Addresses, and also conferred the Degree of LL.D. upon Lord Kelvin, who then took the chair and conferred the Degree of LL.D. on the following:

Professor CLEVELAND ABBE, Meteorological Office, Washington.

Professor CHRISTIAN CHRISTIANSEN, Copenhagen.

Professor PER THEODOR CLEVE, University of Upsala.

General ANNIBALE FERRERO, Ambassador from H.M. the King of Italy.

Professor IZIDOR FROHLICH, University of Buda-Pest.

Professor Gabriel Lippmann, La Sorbonne, Paris.

Professor Archibald Liversidge, University of Sydney, New South Wales.

Professor Éleuthère Mascart, Collége de France, Paris.

Professor Henri Moissan, University of France, Paris.

Professor Simon Newcomb, Johns Hopkins University, Baltimore.

Professor Nicolas Oumov, University of Moscow.

Professor Emile Picard, University of France, Paris.

Professor Georg Quincke, University of Heidelberg.

Professor Woldemar Voigt, University of Göttingen.

Lord Kelvin then said,—The University of Glasgow is honoured by the presence to-day of many distinguished visitors from distant countries, from America, from India, from Australia, and from all parts of the United Kingdom. Names of men renowned for their scientific work in foreign lands have been added to our list of honorary graduates. That I have had the honour of conferring these degrees in the name of the University is a subject of keenest regret to all here present, because it is due to the absence of Principal Caird, on account of illness. We hope that the beginning of next session will see him at home in the University with thoroughly recovered health. In his absence the duty of conferring degrees has fallen, according to University law, on me as senior Professor present.

I am also one of the recipients of the degrees, and, in the name of all who have to-day been created Doctors of Laws of the University of Glasgow, I thank the Senate for the honour which we have thus received on the occasion of the Jubilee of my professorship. For myself, I can find no words to express my feelings on this occasion. My fifty happy years of life and work as Professor of Natural Philosophy here, among my students and my colleagues of the University, and my many kind friends in the great city of Glasgow, call for gratitude; I cannot think of them without heartfelt gratitude. But now you heap coals of fire on my head. You reward me for having enjoyed for fifty years the privilege of spending my time on the work most congenial to me and in the happiest of surroundings.

You could not do more for me if I had spent my life in hardships and dangers, fighting for my country, or struggling to do good among the masses of our population, or working for the benefit of the people in public duty voluntarily accepted. I have had the honour to receive here to-day a gracious message from His Royal Highness the Prince of Wales, and addresses from sister universities in all parts of the world; from learned societies, academies, associations, and institutions for the advancement of pure and applied science; from municipal corporations and other public bodies; from submarine telegraph companies, and from their officers, my old comrades in their work; from students, professors, and scientific workers of England, Scotland, and Ireland, and other countries, including my revered and loved St. Peter's College, Cambridge.

I have had an address also from my twenty Baltimore co-efficients of 1884. The term "coefficients" is abused by mathematicians. They use it for one of the two factors of the result. To me the professor and his class of students are coefficients, fellow-workers, each contributing to whatever can possibly be done by their daily meetings together. I dislike the term *lecture* applied here. I prefer the French expression "conference." I feel that every meeting of a professor with his students should be rather a conference, than a pumping-in of doctrine from the professor perhaps ill understood and not well received by his students. The Scottish Universities have enabled us to carry out this French idea of conference. I think in every one of his classes the professor is accustomed to speak to his students, sometimes in the form of *viva voce* examination, and oftener, I hope, in the manner of interchange of thoughts, the professor discovering whether or not the student is following his lecture, and the student, by showing what he knows or does not know, helping the professor through his treatment of the subject.

I have had interesting and kindly addresses from my old Japanese students of Glasgow University, now professors in the University of Tokyo, or occupying posts in the Civil Service and Engineering Service of Japan. I wish particularly also to thank my Baltimore coefficients for their address. They have been useful to myself in my own keen endeavour—unsuccessful, I must say, nevertheless keen—to find out something definite and clear about light and ether and crystals.

The addresses which I have received to-day contain liberal and friendly appreciation of all my mathematical and physical papers, beginning in 1840 and ending—not yet I hope. The small proportion of that long series of writings which has led to some definite advancement of science is amply credited for its results. A larger part, for which so much cannot be said, is treated with unfailing and sympathetic kindness as a record of persevering endeavour to see below the surface of matter. It has been carried on in the faith that the time is to come when much that is now dark in physical science shall be seen bright and clear, if not by ourselves, by our successors in the work.

I am much gratified by the generous manner in which these addresses have referred to the practical applications of science in my work for submarine telegraphy; my contributions to the advancement of theoretical and practical knowledge of the tides; my improvement in the oldest and next oldest of scientific aids to navigation—the sounding plummet and the mariner's compass; and my electric measuring instruments for scientific laboratories, for the observation of atmospheric electricity, and for electric engineering.

I now ask the distinguished men who have honoured me by presenting to me these addresses, to accept for themselves personally, and for the societies represented by them, my warmest thanks for the great treasure which I have thus received—good-will, kindness, friendship, sympathy, encouragement for more work—a treasure of which no words can adequately describe the value.

I cordially thank the French Academy of Sciences for their great kindness in sending me by the hands of my loved and highly esteemed colleague, Mascart, the Arago Medal of the Institute of France.

I thank all present in this great assembly for their kindness which touches me deeply; and I thank the City and University of Glasgow for the crowning honour of my life which they have conferred on me by holding a commemoration of the Jubilee of my professorship.

Professor Mascart's Address.

Professor Mascart, who was the delegate of Le College de France and L'Académie des Sciences, Paris, at the Jubilee, had intended to make the following speech when presenting the Arago Medal. He afterwards gave his MS. to Lady Kelvin, and said that he had been too much touched by the ceremony to be able to deliver his address.

Milord et cher confrère,—L'Académie des Sciences de Paris, dans laquelle vous êtes aujourd'hui le doyen des associés étrangers, a voulu se joindre aux savants de tous les pays du monde, à vos admirateurs, à vos amis, pour vous apporter des felicitations chaleureuses à l'occasion du cinquantenaire de votre arrivée comme professeur à l'Université de Glasgow que vous avez tant illustrée.

Il y a quelques mois, l'Institut de France célébrait le centième anniversaire de sa fondation, ou plutôt de la reconstitution des anciennes Académies sur des bases plus larges. Nous ne pouvons oublier l'élévation de langage avec laquelle le Président de la Société Royale de Londres vint alors traduire les sentiments de cordialité de cette grande et célèbre Institution.

Dans une autre réunion, ou vous parliez en votre nom personnel, vous nous avez causé une profonde émotion en déclarant que vous aviez une dette de reconnaissance envers notre pays, que nos grands esprits tels que Fourier, Laplace et Sadi Carnot avaient été vos inspirateurs et que vous considériez la France comme l' "alma mater" de votre jeunesse scientifique.

Si la dette existe, vous l'avez payée avec usure. Dans la longue série de travaux et de découvertes qui galonnent votre admirable carrière, une des plus nobles que l'on puisse rêver, vous avez abordé toutes les questions de cette science à laquelle la littérature anglaise conserve le beau nom de "philosophie naturelle," soit pour contribuer aux progrès des conceptions théoriques, soit pour en déduire des applications utiles au développement de l'industrie et au bien de l'humanité.

Quoi que l'avenir réserve au génie inventif de l'esprit humain, votre nom restera comme ayant été le guide le plus sur dans une époque féconde et le véritable éducateur de la génération actuelle dans le domaine de l'électricité.

Je suis particulièrement heureux que l'Académie des Sciences m'ait confié le soin de vous remettre une médaille d'or à l'effigie d'Arago, médaille qu'elle réserve pour rendre hommage aux services exceptionnels rendus à la science et qui porte cette devise: "Laudes damus posteri gloriam."

Vos confrères de l'Institut de France espèrent que vous voudrez considérer ce souvenir comme un témoignage de haute estime et de leurs sentiments les plus affectueux.

Dans une circonstance à laquelle je faisais tout à l'heure allusion, vous avez rappelé aussi qu'au début de votre carrière vous aviez fréquenté les laboratoires du College de France, où les professeurs de cette époque, Biot, Lionville et Victor Regnault accueillirent avec empressement le jeune homme dont les premières publications faisaient déjà prévoir le brillant avenir.

L'Assemblée de Professeurs du College a bien voulu, par une délibération spéciale, me confier la mission de vous témoigner le prix qu'elle attache à ce souvenir en vous apportant le tribut de ses cordiales félicitations.

J'ai encore comme Président actuel de la Société d'Encouragement pour l'Industrie Nationale, à vous traduire les hommages de cette association, fondée à l'origine du siècle et qui a pour but de faciliter l'application des découvertes scientifiques aux progrès industriels.

Il y a deux ans, la Société avait l'honneur de vous décerner l'une de ses plus hautes récompenses, par l'attribution d'une médaille de platine à l'effigie d'Ampère. Vous estimerez sans doute que les figures d'Arago et d'Ampère, placées côte à côte dans la collection de vos écrins, ne s'y trouveront pas en mauvaise compagnie, de même que les deux savants ont été associés de si près dans leurs immortelles découvertes.

Enfin vous avez eu à diverses reprises l'occasion de témoigner une bienvaillance particulière à la Société Internationale des Électriciens en assistant à quelques unes de ses séances et en honorant de votre concours le Congrès de 1889.

La Société m'a prié d'être son interprète dans la circonstance actuelle, pour vous exprimer ses sentiments de reconnaissance, son admiration pour vos travaux, et pour vous offrir des respectueux hommages.

Banquet in St. Andrew's Hall

On the evening of Tuesday, June 16, Lord Kelvin was entertained by the Corporation and University of Glasgow at a banquet in St. Andrew's Hall. The large company, like the earlier gatherings associated with the Jubilee, was representative of the science and philosophy of the world.

After dinner, Sir James Bell, Bart., the Lord Provost, who presided, read a message from the Queen as follows:

The Queen commands me to beg that you will kindly express to Lord Kelvin Her Majesty's sincere congratulations on the occasion of the Jubilee of his professorship in the Glasgow University. Her Majesty trusts that many years of health and prosperity may be in store for him and Lady Kelvin. The Queen is particularly gratified at the presence of so many eminent representatives from all countries of the world, who have come to do honour to your distinguished guest.

ARTHUR BIGGE, on behalf of
HER MAJESTY.

The Lord Provost, on rising to propose the toast of the evening, was received with prolonged applause. He said,—We have received one or two cable messages which I have been desired to read. They are addressed to Lord Kelvin. The first is from Toronto, and reads as follows: "The Councils of the University of Toronto and of University College offer you their heartiest congratulations on your attainment of your fiftieth year of your professorship, and they earnestly wish that you may be long spared to serve science, whose advancement you have so signally promoted. J. Lowden, president." Then from Quebec there is one:—"I send most cordial congratulations on this occasion. Your illustrious fifty years' services have been of great profit to science.—La Flamme." Another telegram, just received from Moscow, is addressed: "To the celebrated Lord Kelvin, famous, learned, we send our congratulations.—The Moscow University students." In addition to these telegrams, I have been requested to say that numerous letters have been received expressing, on behalf of the writers, regret at inability to be present at these celebrations. I have one from Lord Salisbury expressing his great regret. Mr. Campbell has intimated one that he has had from Sir John Gorst, and there are many others. I wish to read one from Principal Caird. Need I say how greatly we all regret the cause by which we are unavoidably deprived of his presence, and of the matchless eloquence with which he would have presented the toast which in his absence falls to me to-night.

THE UNIVERSITY, GLASGOW,
June 10, 1896.

MY DEAR SIR JAMES,

Will you allow me to express to you, and to any others who may chance to notice my absence, my great disappointment and regret that I am not permitted to be present next week at the banquet at which you are to preside, or at any of the other functions in connection with Lord Kelvin's Jubilee. It would have been a great gratification to me to take part in the universal tribute of admiration and respect that is to be paid to the great man of science, and to give public expression to the esteem and affection which for many a long year I have felt for him as my colleague and friend. Acting under medical advice, however, I am reluctantly constrained owing to a recent illness, from which I have not yet completely recovered, to refrain from taking part in the approaching ceremonials.

Very truly yours,

J. CAIRD.

I know how far more deeply than can be expressed in words our beloved Principal grieves over his inability to be with us to-night, but we confidently hope that he may soon again be restored to health.

Ladies, my Lords, and Gentlemen,—The toast that I have now the honour to propose for your acceptance is that of "Lord Kelvin, and hearty congratulations on the attainment of his professorial Jubilee." These congratulations are manifold and great—they come from all European countries; they come from India and our Colonies, from across the Atlantic, from the great scientific societies and from the leading scientists of to-day; and in this City we are doing what is for us unique—the University and City authorities are joining hand in hand to show, in the strongest manner possible, our intense admiration and appreciation of Lord Kelvin and his work. My Lords and Gentlemen, if we turn to consider why we are honouring ourselves by paying this tribute to the worth of our fellow-citizen, and the only citizen who has received this city's freedom, we are confused with the almost numberless reasons that could be given, any one of which would be amply sufficient to inspire us to give honour to whom so much honour is due. Since Lord Kelvin as a student in Cambridge, in 1845, attained distinction as Second Wrangler and First Smith Prizeman, his life has been devoted to science and over such large and varied fields of research that it would be impossible to even name these or the discoveries he has made, but we cannot but let our memory carry us back to what we know or have read of those events in Lord Kelvin's life which are now world's history. We know the part Lord Kelvin took in laying the Atlantic cable; and when others, amid innumerable trials, lost heart, he never faltered in the belief that all difficulties could and would be overcome; and the discoveries he made regarding the "law of squares," the mirror galvanometer, the siphon recorder, materially helped in the working-out of this triumph of science. A great social and commercial revolution dates from August, 1858, when the message was signalled under the ocean, 'Europe and America are united by telegraphic communication. Glory to God in the highest, on earth peace and goodwill towards men.'

To almost every branch of scientific research Lord Kelvin has given contributions of inestimable value. In regard to the laws of heat, he has been one of the greatest discoverers; while, through the perfecting of the compass and improving the means of sounding, the risk of loss of life or vessel has been so minimised that I do not think I am over-stating the case when I say that these two discoveries have saved thousands of lives, and millions of pounds worth of property. In regard to electrical science Lord Kelvin is known the world over as the greatest authority; while his knowledge of the laws of electricity, and his singular faculty in applying his knowledge to the practical purposes of our daily life, has gained him a position above all others. But, my Lords and Gentlemen, we may ask how so much has been accomplished and achieved? We have known of great mathematicians who could solve most difficult problems, and we have known others who have laid bare secrets of nature. In what way did they differ from our guest in the methods of their research?

In answer, may I quote the words of Professor Helmholtz: 'He has striven with great consistency to purify the mathematical theory from hypothetical assumptions which were not a pure expression of the facts. In this way he had done very much to destroy the old natural separation between experimental and mathematical physics, and to reduce the latter to a precise and pure expression of the laws of phenomena. He is an eminent mathematician, but the gift to translate real facts into mathematical equations, and *vice versa*, is by far more rare than that to find the solution of a given mathematical problem, and in this direction Sir William Thomson is most eminent and original.' These words were written over twenty years ago; and true as they were then, Lord Kelvin's life has shown these qualities to be fixed and abiding principles of his mind. He has never loved abstract theories for themselves alone, but has ever striven to solve problems, that he might apply the solution to practical use and to the furthering of our well-being. How much this great genius has accomplished we may fail to realise, but we do recognise in Lord Kelvin one who has been given mental gifts and graces such as are vouchsafed to a few in any century, and these gifts have been consecrated with unceasing industry to the good of mankind. When we extend our hearty congratulations, from a university point of view, we do so full of gratitude for the great distinction such a life has brought to our ancient seat of learning; from a civic point of view, from the honour it has brought to our city; and, when we turn to the scientific, we find representatives of nations and learned societies vying with each other to do honour to one who has laid such a foundation of discovery for others to build on.

Lord Kelvin's discoveries and appliances have world-wide use, from the most complicated and delicate instrument to improvements on the simplest form of mechanism. His industry is unwearied, and he seems to take rest by turning from one difficulty to another—difficulties that would appal most men, and be taken as enjoyment by no one else. But what has been the result of these great gifts of genius, coupled with this industry? They have resulted in a lifetime of discoveries fraught with good; year by year something has been accomplished; paper after paper that are standards on their subject-matter have been written until we are lost in amazement at what has been done. While concurrently with this active productivity his lordship's university classes have been carefully carried on. How many students in these fifty years of Jubilee have been fired with their teacher's enthusiasm we can never know, but from this class many have gone who have attained great distinction, and who look back with pride and pleasure to the days passed in the Natural Philosophy class-room of Glasgow University.

My Lords and Gentlemen, it is given to few men to labour in one place for fifty years; it is given to almost none to do so with the distinction achieved by our guest, a distinction now so great that he may justly be called the greatest living scientist. Lord Kelvin has given in America the Baltimore lectures—lectures not given to students but to professors. He was a member of the Niagara Commission. He has been awarded honours innumerable and of every kind from learned societies in the Old World and the New, and, as you know, he has just demitted the office of President of the Royal Society, after a term of office marked by the greatest brilliancy. This life of unwearied industry, of universal honour, has left Lord Kelvin with a lovable nature that charms all with whom he comes in contact.

Unaffected, ever wishful to get the opinions of others, courteous and kind, well might Professor Huxley, after a memorable controversy, introduce Lord Kelvin as his successor in the presidency of the British Association with these words: 'Gentler knight never broke lance.' Lord Kelvin, indeed, inspires love and reverence in all. His home life is love and melody. His helpmate is worthy of him, and greater cannot be said. Those who have the great privilege of their friendship, with fervent prayer, will in their hearts add to the toast the wish that Lord and Lady Kelvin may long be spared to one another.

Lord Kelvin, who on rising to reply was greeted with prolonged applause, said,—First of all, I desire to express the deep and heartfelt gratitude with which I have heard the most kind and gracious message from Her Majesty the Queen, which has been read to us by the Lord Provost. But I cannot find words for thanks. I can only, on the part of Lady Kelvin and myself, tender an expression of our loving loyalty to the Queen. My Lord Provost, my Lords, and Gentlemen, I thank you with my whole heart for your kindness to me this evening. You have come here to commemorate the Jubilee of my University professorship, and I am deeply sensible of the warm sympathy with which you have received the kind expressions of the Lord Provost regarding myself in his review of my fifty years' service, and his most friendly appreciation of practical results which have come from my scientific work.

I might perhaps rightly feel pride in knowing that the University and City of Glasgow have joined in conferring on me the great honour of holding this Jubilee, and that so many friends and so many distinguished men,—friends and comrades, day-labourers in science—have come from near and far to assist in its celebrations, and that congratulations and good wishes have poured in on me by letter and telegram from all parts of the world. I do feel profoundly grateful. But when I think how infinitely little is all that I have done I cannot feel pride; I only see the great kindness of my scientific comrades, and of all my friends in crediting me for so much.

One word characterises the most strenuous of the efforts for the advancement of science that I have made perseveringly during fifty-five years; that word is FAILURE. I know no more of electric and magnetic force, or of the relation between ether, electricity, and ponderable matter, or of chemical affinity, than I knew and tried to teach to my students of natural philosophy fifty years ago in my first session as Professor. Something of sadness must come of failure; but in the pursuit of science, inborn necessity to make the effort brings with it much of the *certaminis gaudia*, and saves the naturalist from being wholly miserable, perhaps even allows him to be fairly happy in his daily work.

And what splendid compensation for philosophical failures we have had in the admirable discoveries by observation and experiment on the properties of matter, and in the exquisitely beneficent applications of science to the use of mankind with which these fifty years have so abounded! You, my Lord Provost, have remarked that I have had the good fortune to remain for fifty years in one post. I cordially reply that for me they have been happy years. I cannot forget that the happiness of Glasgow University, both for students and professors, is largely due to the friendly and genial City of Glasgow, in the midst of which it lives. To live among friends is the primary essential of happiness; and that, my memory tells me, we inhabitants of the University have enjoyed since first I came to live in it (1832) sixty-four years ago. And when friendly neighbours confer material benefits, such as the citizens of Glasgow have conferred on their University in so largely helping to give it its present beautiful site and buildings, the debt of happiness due to them is notably increased.

I do not forget the charms of the old college in the High Street and Vennel, not very far from the comforts of the Salt-market. Indeed, I remember well when, in 1839, the old Natural Philosophy class-room and apparatus-room (no physical laboratory then) was almost an earthly paradise to my youthful mind; and the old College Green, with the ideal memories of Osbaldistone and Rashleigh and their duel, created for it by Sir Walter Scott, was attractive and refreshing to the end. But density of smoke and of crowded population in the adjoining lanes increased, and the pleasantness, healthiness, and convenience of the old college, both for students and professors, diminished year by year. If, my Lord Provost, your predecessors of the Town Council, and the citizens of Glasgow, and well-wishers to the city and its University all over the world, and the government, and the great railway company that has taken the old college, had left us undisturbed on our ancient site, I don't believe that attractions elsewhere would have taken me away from the old college; but I do say that twenty-five of the fifty years of professorship which I have enjoyed might have been less bright and happy, and I believe also less effective in respect to scientific work, than they have been with the great advantages with which the University of Glasgow has been endowed since its migration from the High Street.

My Lord Provost, I ask you to communicate to your colleagues of the Town Council my warmest thanks for their great kindness to me in joining to celebrate this Jubilee. Your Excellency, my Lords and Gentlemen, I thank you all for the kind manner in which you have received the toast of my health proposed by the Lord Provost, and for your presence this evening to express your good wishes for myself.

Professor Sir W. T. Gairdner, in proposing the toast of the Representatives present from other Universities and learned bodies, spoke of Lord Kelvin's personal character as it had appeared to his colleagues, and said: 'I feel very strongly that all that has been said of the scientific eminence of Lord Kelvin and of his innumberable and most remarkable discoveries in science leaves still without emphasis one point about him which only those who have been in close association with him can appreciate, and that is his childlike humility of character — his very remarkable power of inspiring affection as well as esteem, his interest and sympathy with every one who is related to him in any way whatever.'

His Excellency General Annibale Ferrero, Lord Lister, and Professor Simon Newcomb of Washington responded to this toast; and among the later speakers were Professor Story, the Earl of Rosse, Sheriff Berry, and Sir Henry Roscoe.

The University Senate had arranged that the celebrations should terminate on Wednesday with a sail through some of the more picturesque parts of the Clyde. On the invitation of the Senate, a company of about two hundred and fifty, including Lord and Lady Kelvin and a large number of the delegates and visitors attending the celebrations, as well as the officials of the University, assembled at St. Enoch's Station, and were conveyed by special trains to Princes Pier, Greenock, where they embarked on board the steamer 'Glen Sannox.' The route followed was by Largs and Millport, and then northwards along the western coast of the Island of Bute, through the Kyles, and thence homeward by Princes Pier.

List of Guests

Invited by the University and City of Glasgow to take part in the Celebration of the Jubilee of Lord Kelvin

Aall, Cato, Christiania.
Abbe, Prof. Cleveland, Weather Bureau, Washington.
Abel, Sir Fred., 2 Whitehall Court, London, S.W.
Abercromby, Lord, 14 Grosvenor St., London, W.
Abney, Capt. W. de W., C.B., F.R.S., Sc. and Art Dep., London.
Adams, Prof. W. G., D.Sc., King's College, London.
Adamson, James, I.M.E., 58 Romford Rd., London, E.
Adamson, Prof., 4 The College, Glasgow.
Adamson, Rev. Thomas, 3 Doune Terrace.
Addie, John, Viewpark, Uddingston.
Addison, W. Innes, 19 Hartington Gds., Dowanhill.
Aitken, John, F.R.S., Darroch, Falkirk.
Alison, Gen. Sir A., Bart., Woodville, Colinton.
Allan, F. W., 125 Buchanan Street.
Alley, Stephen, Langside House, Langside.
Alexander, Bailie, 339 Bath Street.
Alexander, G. W., M.A., 129 Bath Street.
Alexander, Thos., 8 Lorraine Gardens.
Alston, J. Carfrae, 9 Lorraine Gardens.
Ames, Jos. S., Ph.D., Johns Hopkins Univ., Baltimore.
Anderson, Alex. P., Redhall, Kelvinside.
Anderson, Rev. John, B.D., 72 Montgomerie St.
Anderson, John, Jr., D.L., J.P., 18 Park Circus.
Anderson, Prof. M'Call, 2 Woodside Terrace.
Anderson, Robt., 2 Belhaven Terrace.
Anderson, Coun. Robert, 50 Queen Mary Avenue.
Anderson, Dr. Wallace, 23 Woodside Place.
Anderson, Wm. C., B.Sc., Mavisbank, Partickhill.
Anderson, Coun. W. F., Flemington, Kenniahead.
Anderson, W. F. G., 47 Union Street.
Angellier, Professor, Lille.
Arnot, Wm., 21 Lansdowne Crescent.
Arnott, Sir John, D.L., Woodlands, Cork.
Arrol, Sir W., LL.D., M.P., Seafield, Ayr.
Arthur, Allan, Calcutta.
Arthur, John W., 2 West Regent Street.
Arthur, Matthew, Fullarton, Troon.
Arthur, Mrs. Barshaw, Paisley.
Asher, Rt. Hon. Alex., M.P., Edinburgh.
Ashton, Rev. J. P., M.A., Bloomfield St., London.
Austen, W. C. Roberts, C.B., Royal Mint, London.
Ayrton, Prof., City and Guilds Cent. Tech. Coll., London.

Bain, Sir James, 3 Park Terrace.
Bain, Andrew, 17 Athole Gardens.
Baird, William, Elie House, Elie, Fife.
Baird, J. G. A., M.P., Muirkirk.
Baird, Allan F., 147 St. Vincent Street.
Baker, Sir Benjamin, 2 Queen Square Pl., London.
Balfour, Prof. Bayley, University, Edinburgh.
Balfour, Sheriff, 2 Northpark Terrace.
Ball, Prof. Sir R. S., King's College, Cambridge.
Balmain, Michael, 25 Belhaven Terrace.
Balmain, Thomas, 1 Kew Terrace.
Bannatyne, Mark, 15 Windsor Terrace, W.
Bannatyne, Miss, 15 Windsor Terrace, W.
Barclay, H. C., M.D., 39 Kersland Terrace.
Barker, Prof. G. F., M.D., U.S.A.
Barlow, John, M.D., 4 Somerset Place.
Barnwell, Richard, Fairfield, Govan.
Barr, Dr. Thomas, 13 Woodside Place.
Barr, Prof., Royston, Dowanhill, Glasgow.

Barrett, F. T., Hollybank, Crow Road, Partick.
Bathgate, Wm., H.M.I.S., 13 Westbourne Gardens.
Battersby, Councillor, 187 West George Street.
Beardmore, Wm., Montgomerie House, Kelvinside.
Beatson, Dr., 7 Woodside Crescent.
Becker, Prof., Observatory, Dowanhill, Glasgow.
Bell, Sir James, Bart., Lord Provost, 7 Marlborough Terrace.
Bell, John, at 7 Marlborough Terrace.
Bell, Henry, 39 Fitz-John's Avenue, London.
Bell, A. M., Limpsfield, Rawlinson Road, Oxford.
Bergin, Prof. W., M.A., Queen's College, Cork.
Berry, Sheriff, LL.D., 5 University Gardens.
Bilsland, Councillor, 28 Park Circus.
Bilsland, John, 9 Park Quadrant.
Binnie, Robert, Uddingston.
Binnie, Thomas, 3 Park Gate.
Bird, Robert, 58 Renfield Street.
Black, Wm. G., 12 Sardinia Terrace.
Black, Rev. James, D.D., 13 South Park Terrace.
Blackburn, Miss, Killearn House, Killearn.
Blackburn, John, 3 Park Circus Place.
Blackie, Principal, 1 Belhaven Terrace.
Blackie, W. W., B.Sc., 6 Thornville Terrace.
Blackie, Jas. R., Northbank, Dowanhill.
Blacklock, Miss Isabella, M.A., Hallhill, Baillieston.
Blair, G. M'Lellan, 2 Lilybank Terrace.
Blair, Miss S. L., M.A., Kilwinning.
Blandy, J. Ernest, Piccadilly, London.
Blantyre, Lord, Erskine, Bishopton.
Blyth, Robert, 1 Montgomerie Quadrant.
Blyth, Prof. James, 170 Great Western Road.
Blythswood, Lord, Blythswood House, Renfrew.
Boltzmann, Prof. Dr. Ludwig, Vienna.
Bond, W. G., Editor *Electrician*, London.
Bottomley, A. W. T., 13 University Gardens.
Bottomley, Dr. J. T., 13 University Gardens.
Bottomley, Wm., 15 University Gardens.
Bower, Prof., 45 Kersland Terrace.
Bowser, Chas. H., 12 Ure Place, Montrose Street.
Bowser, Howard, 13 Royal Crescent, W.
Boyd, D. R., B.Sc., Mason College, Birmingham.
Boyd, James, The Hall, Thorntonhall.
Boyd, Rev. A. K. H., D.D., St. Andrews.
Boyd, Rev. Wm., LL.D., 6 Park Circus Place.
Bradley, Prof., 10 Bruce Street, Hillhead, Glasgow.
Braid, Francis, 32 Westbourne Gardens.
Brailsford, H. N., M.A., 31 Bank Street.
Bramwell, Sir F. J., Bart., D.C.L., 5 Great George Street, London.
Brand, James, 10 Marchmont Terrace.
Bremen, Herr Louis von, c/o D. M. Stevenson.
Bremner, Rev. Dr., Northfield, Partick.
Brechin, Councillor, Gartmore, Pollokshields.
Breen, George, Broomhill, Partick.
Brodie, Robert, 23 Belhaven Terrace.
Brown, A. Hargreaves, M.P., 12 Grosvenor Gardens, London.
Browne, George, Beechhill, Crosshill.
Brown, Hugh, Lord Dean of Guild, 9 Clairmont Gds.
Brown, John, M.A., 46 Granby Terrace.
Brown, M. T., 194 St. Vincent Street.
Brown, Prof. A. Crum, 8 Belgrave Cres., Edinburgh.
Brown, Provost, Renfrew.
Brown, Rev. A. M., B.D., Kirkintilloch.
Brown, Rev. David, 19 May Terrace, Mount Florida.
Brown, Rev. R. Howel, Southpark House, Hillhead.
Bruce, Prof., D.D., 32 Hamilton Park Terrace.
Bryce, T. H., M.B., 2 Buckingham Terrace.
Buchan, Alex., LL.D., F.R.S.E., 42 Heriot Row, Edinburgh.
Buchanan, Prof., 193 Bath Street.
Buchanan, Sir D. C. R. C., K.C.B., of Drumpellier, Coatbridge.
Buchanan, Prof. A. M., M.D., 98 St. George's Road.
Buchanan, George B., B.A., M.B., 193 Bath Street.
Buchanan, R. M., M.B., 9 Burnbank Terrace.
Buchanan, John Y., 10 Moray Place, Edinburgh.
Bunten, Jas. C., Monzie Castle, Crieff.
Burnet, John J., 18 University Avenue.
Burnley, Wm. F., 24 Ainslie Place, Edinburgh.
Burns, Sir John, Bart., Castle Wemyss, Wemyss Bay.
Burns, J. W., B.A., Kilmahew, Cardross.
Burrell, Wm., 4 Devonshire Gardens.
Burrows, R. M., M.A., 21 Kelvinside Terrace, S.
Burt, Bailie, Hollybank, Bothwell.

Caird, Robert, 5 Newark Street, Greenock.
Caird, Provost James, Collingwood, Partick.
Caldwell, James, M.P., House of Commons, London.
Callan, Rev. Hugh, Catrine, Ayrshire.
Cameron, Hector C., M.D., 200 Bath Street, Glasgow.
Cameron, Sir Chas., Bart., M.D., LL.D., Balclutha, Greenock.
Campbell-Bannerman, Rt. Hon. Sir Henry, M.P., 6 Grosvenor Place, London.
Cameron, Prof., 7 Newton Terrace, Glasgow.
Campbell, M. Pearce, 9 Lynedoch Crescent.
Campbell, Councillor Angus, 48 West Regent Street.
Campbell, J. A., LL.D., M.P., Stracathro, Brechin.
Campbell, James, D.L., Tulliechewan Castle, Balloch.
Campbell, Sheriff Vary, 37 Moray Place, Edinburgh.

Campbell, Lady, Garscube House, Maryhill.
Candolle, M. Lucien de, Société des Arts, Geneva.
Cannizzaro, Prof., University, Rome.
Carslaw, H. S., M.A., Park Manse, Helensburgh.
Carslaw, James, M.A., M.B., 400 Great Western Rd.
Carson, James H., 26 Old Broad Street, London.
Carswell, Bailie, Murcia, Pollokshields.
Cassells, Councillor John, Hazelbank, Pollokshields.
Cayzer, C. W., M.P., Ralston, Paisley.
Chalmers, A. K., M.D., 23 Kersland Terrace.
Chapman, General, C.B., Edinburgh Castle.
Charteris, Prof., 3 Kirklee Gardens, Kelvinside.
Cheyne, Sheriff, 13 Chester Street, Edinburgh.
Chisholm, Bailie, 4 Royal Terrace.
Christiansen, Prof. C., Copenhagen.
Clapperton, Alan E., 4 Woodside Terrace.
Clapperton, Alex., 4 Woodside Terrace.
Clark, Col. Wm., 16 Montgomerie Crescent.
Clark, David R., 8 Park Drive, W.
Clark, John, Ph.D., F.C.S., Rockbank, Partick.
Clark, Prof. Henry E., 24 India Street.
Clark, Stewart, Kilnside, Paisley.
Clarke, J. F. Wyllie, Carbeth Guthrie.
Clarke, S. L., 33 South Street, St. Andrews.
Cleland, Councillor, Bonville, Maryhill.
Cleland, Prof., 2 The College.
Cleve, Prof. P. T., University, Upsala.
Clifton, Prof., 3 Bardwell Road, Oxford.
Coats, Archd., Woodside, Paisley.
Coats, Prof., 8 University Gardens.
Coats, Sir T. G., Bart., Ferguslie, Paisley.
Coats, W. A., Skelmorlie Castle.
Cochrane, Hon. T., M.P., London.
Coghill, W. C., 1 Royal Terrace, W.
Colebrooke, Sir E. A., Bart., Abington.
Collins, Wm., Marlybank.
Collins, H. B., B.Sc., Garscadden, New Kilpatrick.
Colville, Arch., 28 Lansdowne Crescent.
Colville, James, D.Sc., 14 Newton Place.
Colville, John, M.P., Motherwell.
Common, A. A., LL.D., 63 Eaton Rise, Ealing.
Conacher, John, Edinburgh.
Connor, J. M., M.A., 61 Albert Road, Crosshill.
Cooper, Chas. A., Editor *Scotsman*, Edinburgh.
Cooper, David, 10 St. Andrew's Drive.
Cooper, Provost F. W., Oban.
Copland, W. R., 20 Sandyford Place.
Cormack, J. D., Yorkshire College, Leeds.
Coste, Jules, 131 West Regent Street.
Costigane, J. T., Hampton House, Ibrox.
Coutts, James, M.A., 84 Braeside Street.
Craig, R. H., Westpark, Skelmorlie.
Craig, Rev. Robert, M.A., 9 Warrender Park Road, Edinburgh.
Craig, Arch., LL.B., 5 Fitzroy Place.
Craik, Sir Henry, K.C.B., Dover House, Whitehall.
Crawford, Councillor, Sunnyside, Lenzie.
Crawford, Daniel, 6 Marchmont Terrace.
Crawford, Earl of, Haigh Hall, Wigan.
Crawford, Lawrence, B.Sc., Mason College, Birmingham.
Cross, Alex., M.P., 14 Woodlands Terrace.
Crum, H. B., 9 Hillhead Gardens.
Crum, W. G., of Thornliebank, 4 West Regent Street.
Crum, Miss, Danefield, Largs.
Cumming, Miss Alice L., M.B., 20 Blythswood Square.
Curphey, Wm. F., 15 Bute Mansions.
Cushney, Prof., M.D., 44 East Madison Street, Ann Arbor, Michigan.
Cuthbert, Councillor, 14 Newton Terrace.
Cuthbert, W., Hillfoot.
Cuthbertson, Sir J. N., LL.D., 25 Blythswood Square.

Dalrymple, Sir Charles, Bart., M.P., 5 Onslow Houses, London.
Dalziel, T. K., M.B., 196 Bath Street.
Darwin, Prof. G. H., F.R.S., Cambridge.
Davidson, Councillor John, Dunira, Bearsden.
Davies, Rev. T. Eynon, 3 Victoria Crescent.
Dawson, Thomas, 248 Bath Street.
Deas, James, 7 Crown Gardens.
Denny, Peter, Dumbarton.
Denny, John M., M.P., Dumbarton.
Devies, Major Kevill, Gordon Highlanders.
Dewar, D., Botanic Gardens.
Dewar, Lord Provost, Perth.
Dewar, Miss Margaret, M.B., Gartnavel.
Dewar, Prof. James, LL.D., F.R.S., Peterhouse, Cambridge.
Dick, Bailie James, 10 Belmont Gardens.
Dick, Councillor J. W., 1 Mary's Place, Maryhill.
Dick, G. Handasyde, 31 Hamilton Drive.
Dickinson, Lowes, 1 All Souls Place, London.
Dickson, Charles Scott, Solicitor-General.
Dickson, J. D. H., M.A., Peterhouse, Cambridge.
Dickson, Preceptor, 17 Park Circus Place.
Dickson, Rev. Prof., D.D., 16 Victoria Crescent.
Dickson, Samuel, Bullitt Building, Philadelphia.
Dobbie, A. B., B.Sc., 1 Wilson Street, Hillhead.
Dodds, J. M., M.A., Peterhouse, Cambridge.
Donald, Thomas F., 14 Huntly Gardens.
Donaldson, Charles, Beechwood, Partick.

Donaldson, Jas., 97 West Regent Street.
Donaldson, Mrs. A., 5 Crown Terrace, Dowanhill.
Donaldson, Peter, 5 Princes Terrace.
Donaldson, W. A., Cochno House, Duntocher.
Douglas, Principal, D.D., 10 Fitzroy Place.
Douglas, Campbell, of Mains.
Douglas, Campbell, 266 St. Vincent Street.
Downie, J. Walker, M.B., 4 Woodside Crescent.
Drew, Alexander, Creggandarroch, Blairmore.
Drummond, Rev. R. S., D.D., 50 Westbourne Gdns.
Du Bois, Prof. H., University, Berlin.
Dubs, C. R., 1 Park Terrace.
Dudgeon, W. J., 4 Park Circus Place.
Duff, John, M.D., 5 Abbey Street, Chester.
Duff, Rev. R. A., Ardenlea, Lenzie.
Duff, Rev. R. S., D.D., 21 Bute Gardens.
Duncan, Alex., B.A., LL.D., 23 Granville Street.
Duncan, J. Dalrymple, Meiklewood, Gargunnock.
Duncan, Ebenezer, M.D., Queen's Park House.
Duncan, Walter, 9 Montgomerie Crescent.
Dundonald, Earl of, 34 Portman Square, London.
Dunlop, John, Borgue, Kirkcudbright.
Dunlop, Nathaniel, 1 Montgomerie Crescent.
Dunlop, Jas., M.D., 16 Carlton Place.
Dunmore, Earl of, 61 Great Cumberland Place, London.
Dunn, A. S., 1 Thornville Terrace.
Dunn, Councillor, 26 Westmuir Street, Parkhead.
Dunn, J. E., Dunmullin, Strathblane.
Dunn, James, Admiralty, London.
Dunn, R. H., 4 Belmont Crescent.
Dunn, Sir W., Bart., M.P., London.
Dunn, W. L., 10 Park Terrace.
Dyer, Dr. Henry, 8 Highburgh Terrace, Dowanhill.
Dykes, W. Alston, Hamilton.

Elder, Mrs., 6 Claremont Terrace.
Elgar, Dr. F., 18 York Terrace, Park, London.
Elliott, Prof. A. C., D.Sc., University Coll., Cardiff.
Evans, Sir John, K.C.B., Hemel Hempstead.
Evans, Evan K., M.A., Bryndderwen, Wales.
Everett, Jos. D., Professor, D.C.L., Belfast.
Ewing, Alex. Crum, Keppoch.
Ewing, Prof. J. A., Langdale Lodge, Cambridge.
Eyre, Archbishop, 6 Bowmont Gardens.

Ferguson, Councillor John, Lenzie.
Fergusson, A. A., 11 Grosvenor Terrace.
Ferguson, A., M.B., 21 Hartington Gardens.
Ferguson, Prof., 13 Newton Place.
Ferguson, T. M., Ayton House, Dowanhill.

Ferrero, General Annibale, Italian Ambassador, London.
Fielden, Miss, Nutfield, Surrey.
Fife, Councillor Wm., 9 Camphside Cres., Langside.
Findlay, Jos., Claremont, Kelvinside.
Finlay, Prof., University, Aberdeen.
Finlay, Councillor, Strathallan, Mount Vernon.
Finlay, Sir R. B., M.P., London.
Finlayson, James, Merchiston, Renfrewshire.
Finlayson, James, M.D., Woodside Place.
Fitzgerald, Prof., D.Sc., Trinity College, Dublin.
Fleming, A. J., M.A., Sheriff Villa, Rutherglen.
Fleming, J. Arnold, Woodburn, Rutherglen.
Fleming, James, Woodburn, Rutherglen.
Fleming, J. B., Beaconsfield.
Flint, Rev. Prof., University, Edinburgh.
Flower, Sir W. H., K.C.B., British Museum.
Forman, Charles, C.E., Strean, Bearsden.
Forrester, James M., 3 Dundonald Road.
Forsyth, Prof. A. R., D.Sc., F.R.S., Trinity College, Cambridge.
Foster, J. E., M.A., 30 Petty Cury, Cambridge.
Foster, Prof. Carey, F.R.S., 18 Daleham Gardens, Hampstead.
Foster, Prof. M., Nine Wells, Cambridge.
Foulis, Wm., City Chambers.
Frankland, Prof., Mason College, Birmingham.
Fraser, M. P., LL.B., 27 Merchiston Cres., Edinburgh.
Freeland, Wm., Editor *Evening Times*, 34 Gartork Street.
Frohlich, Prof. Dr., Budapest.
Fullarton, J. H., D.Sc., Marine Laboratory, St. Andrews.
Fuller, Frederick, 9 Palace Road, Surbiton, London.
Fyfe, John, 7 West George Street.
Fyfe, H. B., 16 Montgomerie Quadrant, Kelvinside.
Fyfe, Peter, Milton Lea, Kilmalcolm.

Gairdner, Prof., The College, Glasgow.
Gairdner, Chas., LL.D., D.L., Broom, Newton Mearns.
Gairdner, C. D., C.A., 5 Belhaven Crescent.
Galbraith, John A., 13 Bute Gardens.
Galbraith, J. L., University Library.
Galbraith, Mrs., 3 Blythswood Square.
Gale, J. M., 18 Huntly Gardens.
Galloway, Miss, Queen Margaret College, Glasgow.
Galt, Alex., B.Sc., Pomona, Helensburgh.
Galt, Hugh, M.B., 8 Ardgowan Terrace.
Garey, Councillor, Ravenslea, Crosshill.
Garvie, Provost A. F., Burgh Office, Dumbarton.

Geikie, Sir Arch., LL.D., 28 Jermyn Street, London.
Gemmell, Samson, M.D., 17 Woodside Place.
Gemmill, James F., M.B., Parklea, Dumbreck.
Gerken, Dr. Nicholas, 6 Westbank Terrace.
Gibb, Elias, 13 Montgomerie Crescent.
Gibb, William, City Chambers.
Gibson, Geo. A., M.A., Technical College, Glasgow.
Gilbert, D. M. Crerar, 3 Great Western Terrace.
Gilchrist, Miss Marion, M.B., 3 Kersland Street.
Gildea, Major-General, 14 Montgomerie Crescent.
Gill Dr., Capetown.
Gilliland, Prof. J. H., M.A., Upper Norwood, London.
Gilman, President D. C., Baltimore.
Gladstone, Dr., F.R.S., 17 Pembridge Sq., London, W.
Glaister, John, M.D., 4 Grafton Place, Glasgow.
Glen, Ninian, M.A., C.A., 107 St. Vincent Street.
Goff, Bruce, M.D., Bothwell.
Goodman, Hyam, M.A., 29 Thistle Street.
Gordon, Jos. G., Queen Anne's Mansions, London.
Gordon, Rev. W., Manse, Braemar.
Gorst, Sir J. E., Q.C., M.P., London.
Gosselet, Prof., Lille, France.
Gourlay, Robert, 11 Crown Gardens.
Gourlay, Robert, 4 Granby Terrace.
Gow, Leonard, Hayston, Kelvinside.
Graham, A. G. Barns, of Craigallian.
Graham, Councillor, 165 Nithsdale Road.
Graham, Donald, Airthrey Castle.
Graham, James, of Carfin, Crossford, Lanark.
Graham, Jas., LL.D., 198 West George Street, Glasgow.
Grahame, James, Edinburgh.
Graham, Robert C., Skipness, Kintyre.
Graham, Wm., C.A., 6 Royal Crescent.
Grant, Col. A. B., 16 S. Frederick Street.
Grant, Mrs., Lethendry Lodge, Grantown.
Grant, Miss, Westhorn, Edinburgh.
Grant, Rev. G. M., Dundee.
Grant, Principal, Kingston, Canada.
Gray, George, 72 Hutcheson St.
Gray, H. St. Clair, M.D., 15 Newton Terrace.
Gray, James, 6 Moray Place.
Gray, John, B.Sc., 11 The College.
Gray, Prof. Andrew, M.A., LL.D., Bangor.
Gray, Thomas, Queen Margaret College, Glasgow.
Gréard, Mons., La Sorbonne, Paris.
Greaves, H. K. A., at Garscadden.
Greenlees, Gavin, 25 Iona Place, Mount Florida.
Greenlees, Matthew, Langdale, Dowanhill Gardens.
Grenfell, Captain R. N., H.M.S. Benbow, Greenock.
Grierson, Henry, Craigend Park, Liberton.
Grieve, Provost John, Motherwell.
Grove, John, Junr., 40 Windsor Terrace.
Guild, J. H., M.A., Edinburgh.
Gunn, Rev. G. G., 9 Granby Terrace.
Gurney, Rev. Prof., College of Science, Newcastle-on-Tyne.
Guthrie, Councillor J. C., Altair, Dumbreck.
Guthrie, Sheriff, LL.D., 36 Mansionhouse Road, Langside.

Hamilton, Councillor, 5 Belmar Terrace, Pollokshields.
Hamilton, John, 22 Athole Gardens.
Hamilton, Lord, of Dalzell, Motherwell.
Hamilton, Rev. Thomas, D.D., LL.D., Queen's College, Belfast.
Hannay, David, 20 Huntly Gardens, Glasgow.
Harris, R. T., M.A., Dublin.
Harris, D. F., M.B., B.Sc., 65 Bank Street.
Harrison, Bishop, 25 Burnbank Gardens.
Harvey, Barnett, Yoker.
Harvey, Robert, 11 Albert Drive, Pollokshields.
Hastie, Prof., The College, Glasgow.
Hawthorne, C. O., M.B., 4 St. Mary's Place.
Hay, R. B., B.L., 94 High Street, Paisley.
Heath, Principal, M.A., D.Sc., Mason College, Birmingham.
Hedderwick, J. D., 2 Clairmont Gardens.
Hedderwick, E. C., 17 Kew Terrace.
Henderson, A. C., 47 Union Street.
Henderson, Andrew, The Linn, Cove.
Henderson, John, Towerville, Helensburgh.
Henderson, John, 4 Crown Terrace.
Henderson, J. B., B.Sc., Yorkshire College, Leeds.
Henderson, Miss, The Linn, Cove.
Henderson, G. G., D.Sc., 25 Kersland Terrace.
Henderson, W. C., B.Sc., 39 Kersland Terrace.
Henderson, Sir William, Aberdeen.
Henderson, William, 4 Windsor Terrace.
Henry, James, City Chambers.
Henry, Matthew, Annachmore House, Clynder, Rosneath.
Herkless, Prof., 24 Montgomerie Street.
Herkomer, Prof., R.A., Lululaund, Bushey.
Herriot, Geo., 24 Moray Place, Strathbungo.
Hicks, Dr. H., F.R.S., Hendon Grove, Hendon, London, N.W.
Higginbotham, C. T., Craigmaddie, Milngavie.
Hinshelwood, James, M.A., M.D., 9 Elmbank St.
Hoggan, Geo. B., 8 Lynedoch Crescent.
Holms, Councillor A. C., 3 Athole Gardens.
Hooker, Sir J. D., K.C.S.I., Sunningdale, Berks.

Hope, Councillor, 5 London Terrace.
Hopkinson, John, F.R.S., 5 Victoria St., London.
Horne, R. S., LL.B., 18 Castle Street, Edinburgh.
Houldsworth, Wm., Rozelle, Ayr.
Houston, Rev. A. M., B.D., Auchterderran, Fife.
Howie, Rev. Robert, 4 Bruce Road.
Hozier, Sir W. W., Bart., Mauldslie Castle.
Hunt, Edmund, 121 West George Street.
Hunter, Councillor, 3 Springhill Terrace.
Hunter, J. J., 15 Sutherland Terrace.
Hunter, J. R., Edinburgh.
Hunter, Rev. Dr., Galashiels.
Hunter, R. H., 2 Park Circus.
Hunter, Rev. John, D.D., 9 University Gardens.
Hurlbatt, Miss, Queen Margaret Hall.
Hutchison, Dr., 199 Renfrew Street.
Hutton, James, C.A., 12 Granby Terrace.

Inglis, John, LL.D., Pointhouse Shipyard.
Ingram, A. Grant, City Chambers.
Ingram, J. K., LL.D., Trinity College, Dublin.
Inslee, W. H., Kilbowie.
Irons, Rev. D. E., Mossknowe, Rutherglen.
Irvine, J. M., LL.B., 40 Northumberland Street, Edinburgh.

Jack, Prof., 10 The College, Glasgow.
Jack, A. A., B.A., 10 The College, Glasgow.
Jack, W. R., B.Sc., M.D., 43 Lansdowne Crescent.
Jack, Bailie, 30 Roslea Drive.
Jacks, Wm., LL.D., Crosslet, Dumbarton.
Jamieson, Prof., 16 Rosslyn Terrace, Kelvinside.
Jardine, Mr. Justice, I.C.S., 34 Lancaster Gate, London, W.
Jenkins, Mrs., Llawrvenny, Kirklee Road.
Johanson, Miss, 248 Bath Street.
Johnston, Alex., M.D., Belvidere Hospital.
Johnston, David, 24 Huntly Gardens.
Jones, Principal J. Viriamu, University of Wales.
Jones, Prof., 1 The College, Glasgow.

Kay, John R., 27 Belhaven Terrace.
Kedie, Robert, 11 Eglinton Drive.
Kennedy, Prof. A. B. W., 14 Old Queen Street, Westminster.
Kent, Prof., M.D., 3 Minard Terrace.
Ker, Charles, C.A., 4 Lorraine Gardens.
Ker, Wm., 1 Windsor Terrace.
Kerr, G. M., 9 Derby Crescent.
Kerr, John G., M.A., 15 India Street.
Kerr, John, LL.D., 15 Royal Terrace, Edinburgh.
Kerr, J. M. M., M.B., 28 Berkeley Terrace.
Kerr, Thomas, Afton Lodge.
Kidd, Rev. Jas., D.D., 3 Ayton Road.
Kidston, Geo. J., Finlaystone.
King, Chas. M., Antermony.
King, Councillor, Tigh Realh, Possilpark.
King, George, 12 Sunderland Terrace, London.
King, Miss, 24 Hamilton Terrace, London.
King, Robert, Levenholme, Herlet.
King, Rev. J. W., D.D., New Kilpatrick.
King, Sir Jas., Bothwell Castle.
King, Prof. Thomas, 110 Hill Street.
Kinnear, Hon. Lord, 2 Moray Place, Edinburgh.
Kirkland, Rev. Alex., 2 Ardgowan Terrace.
Kirkpatrick, A. B., 10 Clairmont Gardens.
Kirkwood, Provost James, Govan.
Knox, D. N., M.B., 10 Woodside Place.
Kyllachy, Hon. Lord, 6 Randolph Crescent, Edinburgh.

Laidlaw, David L., 102 St. Vincent Street.
Laidlaw, Robert, 6 Marlborough Terrace.
Laird, Councillor, 3 Seton Terrace.
Laird, Provost, Partick.
Laird, Sir Wm., 7 Kew Terrace.
Laing, John, Westwood.
Lamberton, Alex., Kirkton House, Pollokshields.
Lamond, Henry, 12 Athole Gardens.
Lamont, Daniel, 11 Abbotsford Place.
Lang, Capt. James, 6 Crown Gardens.
Lang, John, City Chambers.
Lang, Very Rev. J. M., D.D., 5 Woodlands Terrace.
Lang, W. R., B.Sc., 9 Crown Gardens.
Lang, W. H., M.B., Bridge of Weir.
Lang, Wm., Crosspark House, Crow Road.
Lang, Prof. Scott, University, St. Andrews.
Langlands, Councillor, 7 Lorne Terrace, Maryhill.
Lawrence, F. W., B.A., Cambridge Union Society.
Lee, Rev. W. E., M.A., Arkleston Road, Paisley.
Leeds, A. N., 11 Grosvenor Terrace, N.
Legg, A. R., Editor *Daily Record*.
Leiper, Wm., Helensburgh.
Leishman, Mrs., Fairyknowe, Blairmore.
Leith, R. F. C., M.B., 129 Warrender Park Road, Edinburgh.
Levi, Senator G. Montefiore, Brussels.
Lilburn, James, 8 Queen's Gardens.
Lindsay, A. M., 1 Park Gate.
Lindsay, Rev. T. M., D.D., 37 Westbourne Gardens.
Lindsay, Wallace M., M.A., Jesus College, Oxford.
Lippmann, Prof., Paris.

Lister, Lord, M.B., F.R.S., 12 Park Cres., London.
Liversidge, Prof., M.A., F.R.S., 9 Victoria Street, Westminster.
Lockyer, Prof. J. N., F.R.S., Royal College of Science, London.
Lodge, Prof., 10 University Gardens.
Lodge, Prof. O. J., D.Sc., University College, Liverpool.
Lovatelli, Count, at Pollok House.
Low, Rev. Canon, Largs Parsonage.
Low, Sir James, Dundee.
Lumsden, James, of Arden, Alexandria.
Lymburn, James, University Library.
Lyness, Miss Elizabeth D., M.B., 2 Parkview Gardens.

M'Ausland, John, Dumbarton.
Macbrayne, D. Hope, 17 Woodlands Terrace.
Macbrayne, J. B., Glenbranter.
M'Call, James, 6 St. John's Terrace.
M'Callum, J. A., LL.B., 194 Ingram Street.
M'Clean, Frank, LL.D., Rusthall House, Tunbridge Wells.
M'Clelland, A. S., 4 Crown Gardens.
M'Cowan, David, 7 Lynedoch Crescent.
M'Cowan, Dr., University College, Dundee.
M'Culloch, James, City Chamberlain's Office.
M'Cunn, Prof., University College, Liverpool.
M'Cutcheon, Bailie, Helenslea, Myrtle Park.
M'Donald, A. B., City Chambers, 6 Broomhill Avenue.
Macdonald, A. G., 8 Park Circus.
Macdonald, George, 2 St. Bernard's Place.
Macdonald, W. H., 2 Athole Gardens Terrace.
Macdonald, Rt. Hon. Lord Justice Clerk, Edinburgh.
Macewen, Prof., 3 Woodside Crescent.
M'Ewen, Rev. A. R., D.D., 25 Woodside Place.
M'Farlane, Councillor John, 11 Camphill Quadrant.
M'Farlane, James, 8 Princes Gardens.
Macfarlane, G. G., 10 Athole Gardens.
Macfarlane, Walter, 12 Lynedoch Crescent.
Macgeorge, B. B., 20 George Square.
M'Grigor, Alexander, Beechwood, Stirling.
Macguire, Rev. Dr., 160 Renfrew Street.
M'Intosh, Prof., St. Andrews.
M'Intyre, John, M.D., Odiham, Hants.
M'Intyre, John, M.B., 179 Bath Street.
M'Jannett, Miss Jane R. S., M.A., 10 Bothwell Terrace, Shawlands.
Mackay, Dr. Yule, University College, Dundee.
Mackay, Provost David, Portland House, Kilmarnock.
M'Kechnie, W. S., LL.B., Thorndean, Elderslie.
M'Kellar, Councillor John 136 Stirling Road.
M'Kendrick, Prof., 2 Florentine Gardens, Hillhead.
Mackenna, P. F., LL.B., County Buildings, Ayr.
Mackenzie, James, 3 Queen's Gardens.
Mackenzie, Provost Archd., Paisley.
Mackenzie, T. R., 3 Hamly Gardens.
M'Keown, Dr. W. A., 20 College Square, East, Belfast.
Mackill, Robert, 6 Montgomerie Quadrant.
M'Killop, F. G., LL.B., Cranworth House, Hillhead.
Mackinlay, David, 6 Great Western Terrace.
Mackinnon, Jas. D., 31 Bank Street.
Mackintosh, Dr. Donald, 10 Lancaster Road, London.
Mackintosh, D. J., M.B., Western Infirmary.
Mackintosh, Rev. James, 52 Great Clyde Street.
M'Lardy, Councillor, Bishopbriggs.
M'Laren, Hon. Lord, 46 Moray Place, Edinburgh.
Maclay, D. T., 3 Woodlands Terrace.
Maclay, Prof. Alex., Chirinch, Milngavie.
Maclay, Councillor, 7 Eildon Villas.
Maclean, Rev. J., D.D., 189 Hill Street.
Maclean, Dr. Magnus, 8 St. Albans Terrace.
Maclean, Sir Andrew, Viewfield, Partick.
MacLehose, James J., M.A., 7 University Gardens.
MacLehose, Robert, M.A., Westdel, Dowanhill.
MacLehose, Robert, 23 Kelvinside Terrace.
M'Lellan, Archd., 8 Berkeley Terrace.
M'Lelland, Robert, 18 Montgomerie Quadrant.
M'Lennan, James, Newhall, Dowanhill.
M'Lennan, Wm., M.B., C.M., 3 Buckingham Terrace.
Macleod, Lady, Finnary, Shandon.
Macleod, Rev. W. H., B.D., Buchanan Manse.
Macleod, Rev. Donald, D.D., 1 Woodlands Terrace.
Macleod, Rev. John, D.D., Manse, Govan.
Macleod, John M., 4 Park Street, E.
Maclure, Wm., 167 New City Road.
Macmahon, Major P. A., R.A., F.R.S., 52 Shaftesbury Avenue, London.
M'Onie, Andrew, 3 University Gardens.
Macphail, Alex., M.B., 13 Ann Street.
Macpherson, H. S., 4 Park Gate.
M'Pherson, Lauchlan, University.
M'Pherson, Rev. J. F., 46 Margaret Street, Greenock.
M'Phun, Bailie, Springbank House, Garscube Road.
M'Vail, D. C., M.B., 3 St. James' Terrace.
Main, Councillor, 2 Dalziel Drive.
Mair, Rev. Dr., Hawick.
Mair, Sheriff, Airdrie.
Maitland, Sir J. R. G., Bart., 19 Cork St., London.
Mance, Sir Henry, 32 Earl's Court Square, London.
Mann, James, 4 University Gardens.
Mann, John, C.A., 18 Westbourne Gardens.

Mann, John, Junr., M.A., C.A., 188 St. Vincent St.
Mann, Wm., Giffnock.
Manners, Jas. R., Editor *N. B. D. Mail.*
Marr, Hamilton, 24 West Ibrox Terrace.
Marr, Alexander, S.R.C., Aberdeen.
Marshall, J. W., M.A., Aberystwyth.
Martin, Councillor, Tollcross.
Martin, T. C., 203 Broadway, New York.
Marwick, Sir J. D., 19 Woodside Terrace.
Mascart, Prof., Paris.
Mason, Thomas, Craigiehall.
Mathieson, Thomas A., 3 Grosvenor Terrace.
Matthews, Rev. Dr., America.
Maury, Prof. Bonet, Paris.
Mavor, G. A., M.A., S.R.C., Aberdeen.
Mavor, Henry A., 54 Kelvingrove Street.
Maxwell, Col., 8 St. James' Terrace.
Maxwell, Sir Herbert E., M.P., London.
Mayer, John, Strathview, Cathkin Road.
Maylard, A. E., 10 Blythswood Square.
Meikle, Wm., Glassford Street.
Menzies, Hugh, M.A., 8 George Street, Grahamston.
Mercier, Mons. Alf., L. ès L., Geneva.
Merz, Dr., The Quarries, Newcastle.
Michie, A. S., 12 Clairmont Gardens.
Middleton, G. S., M.D., 19 Sandyford Place.
Millar, Rev. David, 9 Bute Mansions.
Millar, W. J., C.E., 145 Hill Street, Garnethill.
Miller, John, Dalfruin, Kelvinside.
Miller, T. P., The Cairns, Cambuslang.
Miller, W. G., LL.B., 39 Albany Street, Edinburgh.
Mills, E. J., D.Sc., 60 John Street.
Milligan, James, M.A., 7 Bothwell Terrace.
Milloy, Provost L., Rothesay.
Minton, Dr., 28 Miller Street.
Mirrlees, J. B., Redlands.
Mitchell, Councillor George, 26 Burgher St., Parkhead.
Mitchell, Campbell W., 18 Kew Terrace.
Mitchell, J. C., 13 Windsor Terrace.
Mitchell, Provost Lewis, Rutherglen.
Mitchell, Alex., 22 Belhaven Terrace.
Mitchell, Rev. John, Shettleston.
Mitchell, Stephen, 29 Westbourne Gardens.
Mitchell, C. G., Old Ballikinrain.
Mitchell, J. O., LL.D., 7 Huntly Gardens.
Mitchell, Wm., 18 Kew Terrace.
Moffett, Sir Thomas, LL.D., Galway.
Moir, Prof., 20 Ann Street.
Moissan, Prof., Paris.
Molloy, Rt. Rev. Monsignor, D.D., D.Sc., 86 Stephen's Green, Dublin.
Moncrieff, Hon. Lord, 15 Great Stuart Street, Edinburgh.
Moncrieff, Hugh, 3 Lorraine Gardens.
Monro, D. B., M.A., Provost of Oriel College, Oxford.
Monro, James G., City Chambers.
Monteith, Robert, Greenbank, Dowanhill.
Monteith, J. C., 1 Beaufy Terrace.
Moore, Alex., C.A., 50 Montgomerie Drive, Kelvinside.
Morrin, Councillor, 79 Parson Street.
Morris, Dr. J. Chiston, Philadelphia.
Morrison, A., 40 Hyndland Street.
Morrison, D., LL.D., 4 Victoria Terrace.
Morrison, Thomas, LL.D., 2 Eldon Terrace.
Morton, John, M.B., 7 Hamilton Street.
Mowat, Provost, Stonehaven.
Mudie, Andrew, *Evening Citizen* Office.
Muir, Rev. P. M'Adam, D.D., The Cathedral.
Muir, J. Stanley, B.Sc., 27 Huntly Gardens.
Muir, Sir John, Bart., Deanston.
Muirhead, Dr. A., 2 Princes Street, Westminster.
Multon, Henry C., San Francisco.
Müller, Prof. Max, 7 Norham Gardens, Oxford.
Munro, G. W., 17 Grosvenor Terrace.
Munro, J. M. M., 136 Bothwell Street.
Murdie, Geo., 1 St. John's Terrace.
Murdoch, Alex., 13 Bothwell Terrace.
Murdoch, J. Barclay, Capelrig, Mearns.
Murray, A. Graham, M.P., Edinburgh.
Murray, Bailie Alex., 4 Princes Square.
Murray, Bailie J., 25 Maxwell Drive.
Murray, David, LL.D., 13 Fitzroy Place.
Murray, Dr. John, F.R.S., 1 Savile Row, London.
Murray, J. R. S., 40 Montgomerie Drive.
Murray, Prof., 5 The College.
Murray, Sheriff, Sundown, Kelvinside.

Nadkarin, Ghanasham Nilkanth, B.A., LL.B., London.
Naish, Reginald T., Collargie, Busby.
Napier, Alex., M.D., 15 Queen Mary Avenue.
Napier, Hon. Col. J. Scott, The Barracks.
Napier, Jas. S., West Kilbride.
Napier, Robert, Yoker.
Napier and Ettrick, Lord, Athenæum Club, London.
Natanson, Prof. Ladislas, Cracow.
Neilson, Col. James, Mossend, Holytown.
Neilson, George, Procurator-Fiscal.
Neilson, George, Crossbasket, High Blantyre.
Nelson, Councillor J. E., Belmont, Pollokshields.
Ness, James, LL.B., 157 St. Vincent Street.

Newcomb, Prof. Simon, Washington.
Nichols, Dr. A., M.A., M'Gill University, Montreal.
Nicol, James, City Chambers.
Nicol, J. Wyllie, M.B., 7 Kersland Terrace.
Nimmo, Jas., 26 Belhaven Terrace.
Niven, Prof., University, Aberdeen.

Oatts, Councillor, Crosshill House, Crosshill.
O'Connor, Henry, Milton House Works, Edinburgh.
Ogilvie, Dr., 6 Blythswood Square.
Orr, Rev. John, 170 Renfrew Street.
Orr, John F., 2 Kelvin Drive.
Orr Ewing, C. L., M.P., Ayr.
Osborne, Councillor, 5 Oakley Terrace.
Ousnov, Professor Nicholaus, Moscow.
Overtoun, Lord, Overtoun, Dumbarton.

Parker, Rev. John, St. Peter's, Tollcross.
Paterson, Arch., 109 Bath Street.
Paterson, Peter, M.B., 10 Sandyford Place.
Paton, And. Brown, Hareshawmuir, Kilmarnock.
Paton, Councillor Walter, Strathenien, Pollokshields.
Paton, D. Noel, M.D., 7 Lauriston Lane, Edinburgh.
Paton, David, LL.D., 1 Minard Terrace.
Paton, Rev. James, 2 Park Quadrant.
Paton, River Bailie J. R., Welkom, Pollokshields.
Pearson, Rt. Hon. Lord, 7 Drumsheugh Gardens, Edinburgh.
Pender, J. Dennison, 11 Old Broad St., London E.C.
Pender, Sir John, 18 Arlington St., London, S.W.
Perignat, Don Jose de, 131 West Regent Street.
Perry, Prof., F.R.S., 31 Brunswick Square, London.
Peterson, Prof., M'Gill University, Montreal.
Pettigrew, Bailie, Maggieard, Pollokshields.
Pettigrew, Prof., University, St. Andrews.
Phillips, C. D. F., M.D., LL.D., 10 Henrietta St., Cavendish Square, W.
Philipson, Prof. G. H., M.D., D.C.L., Newcastle.
Picard, Prof., Paris.
Pinkerton, R. H., M.A., University Coll., Cardiff.
Pinkerton, Surgeon Major-General, M.D., Queen's Park House, Crosshill.
Pinloche, Prof., Lille, France.
Pirie, Prof., University, Aberdeen.
Pirrie, Councillor, 9 Buckingham Terrace.
Playfair, Rt. Hon. Lord, 68 Onslow Gardens, London, S.W.
Porter, Rev. Dr., Master of Peterhouse, Cambridge.
Portland, Duke of, 3 Grosvenor Square, London.
Preece, W. H., General Post Office, London.
Primrose, Councillor, Redholme, Dumbreck.
Pringle, J. H., M.B., 256 Bath Street.
Provan, James, 9 Jane Street.
Purser, Prof., LL.D., Queen's College, Belfast.

Quarrier, Wm., Bridge of Weir.
Quincke, Prof., University, Heidelberg.

Raeburn, W. H., 19 Montgomerie Quadrant.
Rainy, Principal, D.D., 23 Douglas Crescent, Edinburgh.
Ramsay, Prof., F.R.S., University College, London.
Ramsay, Dr. Maitland, 15 Woodside Place.
Ramsey, Robert, Deacon Convener, 14 Park Terrace.
Rankin, Daniel, B.A., 65 Bank Street.
Rankin, James, B.Sc., The Terrace, Bearsden.
Rayleigh, Lord, Terling Place, Witham, Essex.
Reay, Lord, 6 Great Stanhope Street, London, W.
Reddie, J. C., 6 Woodlands Terrace.
Reid, Col. Jas. A., Mugdock Castle.
Reid, Dean Watson, 2 Seton Terrace.
Reid, Andrew, 10 Woodside Terrace.
Reid, Hugh, Belmont, Springburn.
Reid, Thomas, Kilmardinny.
Reid, D., 18 Cambridge Street.
Reid, Wm. L., M.D., 7 Royal Crescent, W.
Reid, Thomas, M.D., 11 Elmbank Street.
Reith, Rev. G., D.D., 37 Lynedoch Street.
Rennie, David, 25 Huntly Gardens.
Rennie, J., 8 Richmond Terrace, Whitehall, London.
Rennie, Rev. James, 16 Lansdowne Crescent.
Renshaw, C. B., M.P., Barochan.
Renton, J. C., M.D., 1 Woodside Terrace.
Renwick, R. Mason, 5 Royal Bank Place.
Reynolds, Prof. Osborne, LL.D., Owen's College.
Richardson, David, Hartfield, Cove.
Richmond, Sir David, Broompark, Pollokshields.
Riley, James, Uddingston.
Ristori, Emanuel, 9 Victoria Street, Westminster.
Ritchie, David, Hopeville, Dowanhill.
Ritchie, G. Mure, B.L., 123 St. Vincent Street.
Roberts, Rev. F. H., 24 Belmont Gardens.
Roberton, Lady, 1 Park Terrace, E.
Roberton, J. S., LL.B., 12 Newton Place.
Roberton, J. D., 1 Park Terrace, E.
Roberts, R. D., M.A., D.Sc., 4 Regent Street, Cambridge.
Robertson, J. M'G., M.B., 26 Buckingham Terrace.
Robertson, Rt. Hon. Lord Justice General, 19 Drumsheugh Gardens, Edinburgh.
Robertson, J. C., J.P., 2 La Belle Place.
Robertson, Wm., Oak Park, Mount Vernon.

Robin, Robert, Castlehill, Hamilton.
Robinson, Col. H. D., Ormidale, Bearsden.
Robinson, T. E., City Chambers.
Rodger, Provost, Port Glasgow.
Rogers, J. C., 3 Lancaster Terrace.
Ronaldson, J. M., 44 Athole Gardens.
Roscoe, Sir H. E., Victoria Park, Manchester.
Ross, James, Bank of Montreal, London.
Ross, J. Callender, 46 Holland Street, London.
Ross, John, M'Gill University, Montreal.
Ross, Richd. G., Ravenslea, Dowanhill.
Ross, David, LL.D., 47 Carnarvon Street.
Rosse, Earl of, Birr Castle, Parsonstown.
Rottenburg, Paul, Holmhurst, Dowanhill.
Rottenburg, F., 8 Kew Terrace.
Routh, Ed. J., D.Sc., Peterhouse, Cambridge.
Rowan, James, 22 Woodside Place.
Rowden, Prof., 204 George Street.
Rowe, Professor, Philadelphia.
Rowlette, R. J., B.A., Trinity College, Dublin.
Roxburgh, H. A., 10 Crown Gardens.
Roxburgh, J. A., 15 Lynedoch Crescent.
Rucker, Prof. A. W., F.R.S., 19 Gledhow Gardens, London.
Russell, Arch., Auchinraith, Bothwell.
Russell, Charles, 11 Buckingham Terrace.
Russell, Dr. J. B., 3 Foremount Terrace, Partick.
Russell, Sir Wm., Adare Manor, Ireland.
Russell, Thomas, Cleveden, Kelvinside.
Ryckevorsel, Dr. Elie van, Rotterdam.

Samuel, John S., City Chambers.
Sandeman, David T., 32 Buckingham Terrace.
Sanderson, Prof. Burdon, 64 Banbury Road, Oxford.
Sanderson, Miss, 248 Bath Street.
Saunders, H., Winchester House, London.
Savill, Thomas D., M.D., 60 Upper Berkeley Street, London.
Schuster, Prof., Owens College, Manchester.
Scott, John, C.B., Hawkshill, Largs.
Scott, D. M., 2 Park Quadrant.
Seijas, Simon, 48 West Regent Street.
Sellar, William, Inland Revenue Office.
Seward, A. C., M.A., Cambridge.
Sexton, Prof., 2 Hillend Gardens.
Shand, Lord, 32 Bryanston Square, London.
Shankland, Provost Dugald, Greenock.
Sharp, Provost Robert, Calder Villa, Coatbridge.
Shaw, Wm., 12 Lynedoch Place.
Shearer, Councillor John, 13 Crown Terrace.
Shepherd, J. W., Carrickarden, Bearsden.

Siemens, Alex., 12 Queen Anne's Gate, London.
Simons, Michael, 206 Bath Street.
Simpson, Prof., 216 West George Street.
Simpson, James, 9 Marlborough Terrace.
Sinclair, River Bailie, Ajmere Lodge, Langside.
Skelton, John, 125 George Street, Edinburgh.
Sliman, Councillor, 59 Stanmore Road, Mount Florida.
Sloan, Samuel, M.D., 5 Somerset Place.
Sloan, Wm., Dunara, Helensburgh.
Smart, Professor Wm., Nunholm, Dowanhill.
Smith, Geo., 75 Bothwell Street.
Smith, Geo., J.P., Sweyney Cliff, Salop.
Smith, J. Parker, M.P., Jordanhill.
Smith, J. M., 11 Bute Gardens.
Smith, Major W. A., 12 Hillsborough Terrace.
Smith, Montague, 9 Rosebery Terrace.
Smith, Wm., of Auchentroig, Buchlyvie.
Smith, Rev. G. Muir, 6 Clarendon Place, Stirling.
Smith, Sir Donald A., K.C.M.G., LL.D., London.
Smith, Maj.-Gen. Sir R. Murdoch, K.C.M.G., 17 Magdala Crescent, Edinburgh.
Smith, Rev. Thomas, Edinburgh.
Smith, Dr. A. Wood, 11 Woodside Terrace.
Snodgrass, Wm., M.B., 11 Victoria Crescent.
Somerville, J. B., 147 St. Vincent Street.
Sorley, Councillor Robert, The Firs, Partickhill.
Spens, John A., 14 Woodside Crescent.
Spens, Sheriff, 1 Prince's Gardens.
Spens, W. G., 2 Westbourne Terrace.
Speirs, A. A., of Elderslie.
Stalker, Rev. Jas., D.D., 6 Clairmont Gardens.
Steel, Rev. John, D.D., 20 Craigpark.
Steele, Councillor, 191 Albert Road.
Steggall, Prof., University College, Dundee.
Stephen, Alex., Kelly, Wemyss Bay.
Sterrett, Prof., J. M., M.A., D.D., Washington.
Steven, Hugh, Westmount, Kelvinside.
Steven, Dr. Lindsay, 34 Berkeley Terrace.
Stevenson, Councillor Wm., Hawkhead, Paisley.
Stevenson, Councillor D. M., 9 Doune Terrace.
Stevenson, J. C., 32 Devonshire Place, London.
Stevenson, John J., M.A., 4 Porchester Gardens, London.
Stevenson, James, Hailie, Largs.
Stevenson, Wm., Wardwell, Kinghorn.
Stewart, Andrew, 17 Park Circus.
Stewart, D., Post Office, Glasgow.
Stewart, Councillor Donald, Shawlands Villa.
Stewart, Councillor P. G., 289 Cathcart Road.
Stewart, David, University, Glasgow.

Stewart, Mrs. A. B., Ascog, Bute.
Stewart, Principal, D.D., St. Andrews.
Stewart, Prof., 18 Annfield Terrace, W.
Stewart, James Reid, D.L., 19 Park Terrace.
Stewart, Major R. King, Murdostoun, Newmains.
Stewart, M. H. Shaw, M.P., Garnock.
Stewart, T. M., LL.B., Albion Crescent.
Stirling-Maxwell, Sir John, Bart., M.P., Pollok.
Stokes, Prof. Sir G. G., LL.D., Lensfield Cottage, Cambridge.
Story, Prof., 8 The College.
Strain, John, C.E., Doonbrae, Ayr.
Stromeyer, C. E., 342 Argyle Street.
Strong, David, D.D., 15 Victoria Crescent.
Strong, Prof. H. A., LL.D., 107 Canning Street, Liverpool.
Stroud, Prof., D.Sc., Yorkshire College, Leeds.
Stuart, Miss Emmeline M., M.B., 23 Belgrave Crescent, Edinburgh.
Stuart, Prof. Moody, 3 The College.
Sutherland, L. R., M.B., 53 Kersland Terrace.
Swan, J. W., 58 Holland Park, London.
Sylvester, Prof. J. J., M.A., D.C.L., New College, Oxford.
Symons, Geo. J., F.R.S., 62 Camden Square, London, N.W.

Taggart, H. R., Gartferry, Chryston.
Tait, Ven. Archdeacon, D.D., Rectory, Moylough.
Talbot, Miss, Mugdock Castle, Milngavie.
Tannahill, Miss A. M., 11 Highburgh Terrace.
Tatlock, R. R., Novara, Albert Place, Stirling.
Taylor, J. M., Northbank, Kelvinside.
Taylor, Rev. W. Ross, D.D., 1 Marchmont Terrace.
Teacher, J. H., M.B., 32 Huntly Gdns., Kelvinside.
Templeton, John S., Knockderry Castle, Cove.
Templeton, Jas., 6 South Park Terrace.
Tennant, Sir Charles, Bart., The Glen, Peeblesshire.
Tennent, Gavin P., M.D., 159 Bath Street.
Thomas, Jas. C., M.D., Founders' Court, London, E.C.
Thompson, Prof. Sylvanus P., Morland, Hampstead.
Thompson, James, 5 Devonshire Gardens.
Thomson, Bailie J. M., Glentower, Kelvinside.
Thomson, Geo. P., 4 Queen's Gardens, Dowanhill.
Thomson, Geo. R., M.B., 306 Bath Street.
Thomson, James, 9 Hamilton Drive.
Thomson, James, M.A., C.E., 22 Wentworth Place, Newcastle.
Thomson, James R., Killermont, Maryhill.
Thomson, John S., Kingarth, Bute.
Thomson, Prof. J. M., King's College, London.
Thomson, Rev. James, 32 Belmont Gardens.
Thomson, Prof. J. J., M.A., 6 Scrope Terrace, Cambridge.
Thomson, G. A., Craigard, Lenzie.
Thorpe, Dr. T. E., 61 Ladbroke Grove, London.
Thring, Major R. A., 8 Foremount Terrace.
Tilden, Prof. W. A., D.Sc., Science and Art Department.
Tillie, Alex., Ph.D., 1 Strathmore Gardens, Hillhead.
Tracey, H. J., 67 St. Vincent Street.
Traill, Dr., 35 Trinity College, Dublin.
Tullis, Jas. T., Anchorage, Rutherglen.
Tulloch, F. G., 30 Ashton Terrace.
Turner, B. D., 14 Kingsborough Gardens.
Turner, Prof. Sir W., University, Edinburgh.

Umov, Prof., University, Moscow.
Ure, Alex., M.P., 26 Heriot Row, Edinburgh.
Ure, John G., Rockbank, Helensburgh.
Ure, John, LL.D., Cairndhu, Helensburgh.
Ure, Robert, LL.B., 81 Bath Street.

Van Amringe, Prof., Columbia College, New York.
Veitch, Mrs., Loaning, Peebles.
Violle, Prof., 89 Boulevard St. Michel, Paris.
Voigt, Prof., Gottingen.

Walker, Hugh, M.A., St. David's College, Lampeter.
Walker, Robert, 45 Cecil Street, Hillhead.
Wallace, Councillor Hugh, 3 Crown Circus.
Ward, Fred., 55 Bishopsgate Street, London.
Ward, Principal, Owens College, Manchester.
Warren, Timothy, 10 Westbourne Terrace.
Watkinson, W. H., 29 Kersland Terrace.
Watson, Councillor Thomas, 9 Belhaven Terrace.
Watson, G. L., 9 Highburgh Terrace.
Watson, Henry A., M.A., M.B., 8 Victoria Crescent.
Watson, John E., 16 Belhaven Terrace.
Watson, Rev. Chas., D.D., Northfield, Largs.
Watson, Sir Renny, 16 Woodlands Terrace.
Watson, Sir John, Bart., Earnock, Hamilton.
Watson, T. L., 8 Woodside Crescent.
Watson, Councillor Edward, Allanbank, Crosshill.
Watt, Alexander, 183 St. Vincent Street.
Watt, Rev. J., D.D., 5 Lansdowne Crescent.
Webb, H. S. Beresford, Norbright, Redhill.
Weir, Mrs., Hillcrest, Partickhill.
Weir, Thomas H., B.D., Hillcrest, Partickhill.
Wells, Rev. James, D.D., 4 Knowe Terrace.
Wenley, R. M., D.Sc., D.Phil., 8 St. Alban's Terrace.
Wharton, Admiral W. J. L., F.R.S., Admiralty.

White, R. C. B., of Ardarroch.
Whitton, James, City Chambers.
Whyte, John, City Chambers.
Whyte, Rev. Alex., B.D., 69 Montgomerie St.
Wickstead, Hartley, at 22 Wentworth Pl., Newcastle.
Wilkie, Robert D., 302 Langside Road.
Williams, A. M., M.A., 13 Annfield Terrace, W.
Willis, John C., M.A., 8 Lawrence Place.
Willock, Councillor, 741 Dalmarnock Road.
Willock, Provost H. D., Burgh Office, Ayr.
Wilson, Bailie Walter, 9 Park Drive.
Wilson, David, 18 Woodside Terrace.
Wilson, P. W., M.A., Cambridge.
Wilson, John, M.P., Craigmount, Kelvinside.
Wilson, John, M.P., Hillhead House.
Wilson, Prof. Woodrow, at 18 Annfield Terrace, W.
Windeyer, Sir Wm., C., M.A., Westminster.
Wingate, John B., 7 Crown Terrace.
Wingate, D. C., 7 Crown Terrace.
Wistar, General Isaac J., Philadelphia.
Workman, Chas., M.D., 5 Woodside Terrace.
Wright, Prof. Patrick, 60 John Street.
Wylie, Alex., M.P., Cordale.

Yellowlees, Dr., Gartnavel.
Young, Alf. A., M.B., 226 Bath Street.
Young, D. J., 128 Park Road.
Young, John, B.Sc., 38 Bath Street.
Young, John, LL.D., Hunterian Museum, University.
Young, John, 88 Renfield Street.
Young, Prof. John, M.D., University.
Young, R. Bruce, M.B., 8 Crown Gdns., Dowanhill.
Young, Rt. Hon. Lord, 28 Moray Place, Edinburgh.
Young, T. Graham, Westfield, West Calder.

18 99
UNIVERSITY PRESS
GLASGOW

www.ingramcontent.com/pod-product-compliance
Lightning Source LLC
Chambersburg PA
CBHW030628270326
41927CB00007B/1352